Egyptian Mythology

LIBRARY OF THE WORLD'S
MYTHS AND LEGENDS

Egyptian Mythology

Veronica Ions

PETER BEDRICK BOOKS
NEW YORK

Half-title page. Amon-Ra with the features of Amenhotep III. Musée du Louvre.

Frontispiece. The goddess Mut.

New revised edition first published in the United States in 1983 by Peter Bedrick Books, New York. *Egyptian Mythology* first published 1965. Completely revised 1968. New revised edition published 1982 by Newnes Books, a division of The Hamlyn Publishing Group Limited. Published by agreement with The Hamlyn Publishing Group Limited.

Copyright © Veronica Ions 1968, 1982

Second printing 1986

ISBN 0-911745-07-6
LC 83-71478
Printed in Yugoslavia

Contents

Cults and Divinities

The great number of ancient temples, pyramids and rock-tombs are a striking feature of present-day Egypt. They are a monumental testimony to the highly evolved system of beliefs which held sway in the valley of the Nile for several millennia; and yet our knowledge of these beliefs is surprisingly incomplete. There is little or no direct evidence about them in any present-day religious derivatives. The archaeological remains – the temples, the pyramids and the contents of the tombs, which include papyri and inscriptions on stone as well as statues of various deities – are our chief source of information.

For various reasons the Egyptians attached importance to building monuments that would last. It has been suggested that the natural preservation achieved by burials in the hot sand first gave them the idea of mummification and of tombs that would withstand the ages. This and their superb artistry have combined to produce for the modern world a great heritage and a full – though as yet imperfectly understood – record of their civilisation and beliefs. Another important source is found in the commentaries of Greek observers, but these are of later date.

The nature of the sources usually leads to three general though not necessarily accurate conclusions: that the ancient Egyptians were preoccupied with death, and therefore gloomy; that in the beliefs and rituals of this most religious people may be found clues to the ultimate mysteries of the universe; and that the Egyptians worshipped animals. The last two conclusions would seem to most modern observers to be contradictory; and, as we shall see, though ancient Egyptian mythology is full of animal figures, animal worship is a misnomer, at least so far as the theologians and educated upper classes were concerned.

As to their preoccupation with death, certainly the Egyptians gave it much thought, but it is best viewed as the obverse of a love of life. Ancient Egypt can be defined as that part of the Nile valley made fertile by the annual floods. It contrasted sharply with the desert lands surrounding it, and nearly all the peoples who entered it through the ages gratefully settled and adopted it as their own. Their earthly conditions were indeed blessed, for the ease with which agriculture, the basis of civilisation, could be practised was readily appreciated by settlers from elsewhere; so favourable were conditions for agriculture that it remained the basis of the economy at every level of civilisation for five or six millennia. The forces of nature in the form of cosmic and nature divinities were consequently objects of Egyptian worship. Water and fertile earth were among the earliest objects of veneration; the sun was not understood to be a fructifying force: its power was evident but it was more to be feared than adored.

The Nile and the fertile earth on its banks were a unifying element in ancient Egypt. At the same time the

Opposite. A colonnade in the temple of Luxor (near Thebes), built during the reign of Amenhotep III, whose capital was at Thebes. His great temple was dedicated to the ithyphallic Amon-Ra. Eighteenth Dynasty.

river's 400-mile length and benefi-
cence both attracted and allowed the
settlement of many separate communities from different parts. Such
communities multiplied especially in
the Delta region, where the branches
of the river divided up the land into
a naturally fissile area. In Upper
Egypt, however, slightly more difficult conditions made large-scale community endeavour rather more
desirable.

Each community tended to have its
own set of beliefs and its own god,
and might take its inspiration from
the local surroundings or from the
ancient gods of other parts of Africa,
of Asia or of the Mediterranean
which were the original homes of the
people. Beliefs might also be affected
by commercial or military contacts
with other peoples. Each community
was led by its god, and military victory was seen as his victory over the
god of the conquered people. Thus
we may speak of political causes for
changed beliefs, but do not necessarily mean by this a calculated or cyn-
ical manipulation of the people's faith
by their rulers. In ancient Egypt might
was right: victory proved moral
superiority.

Victory was not, however, the signal for annihilation of the conquered
god. In most cases it called for assimilation. Thus the conquering god
would take over the functions and
nature of the vanquished deity, who
was declared to be one of his aspects;
or would incorporate him into his
own family or divine group, often a
triad. Such a development might be
encouraged by the priests of the conquered deity, who thus sought to pre-
vent his total extinction. It is easy to
see how such tolerance on the part of
the Egyptians led to the growth of
elaborate mythological explanations
of this flow and development of belief. The conditions in which the
Egyptians lived made them tolerant
and also poetical in their modes of
thought. Even among their theologians logical rigour was little considered. Contradictory myths co-
existed happily, for they were but different aspects of reality: the search
after 'truth' in the modern sense

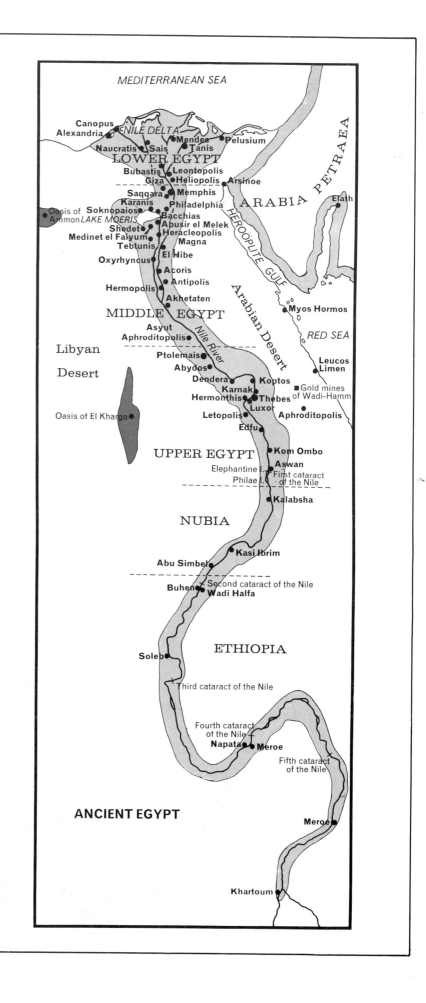

Opposite. The concentration of its cities along the narrow strip of the cultivable river valley emphasises ancient Egypt's dependence on the Nile. Without its waters no community could have existed.

Right. A stela or inscribed memorial stone commemorating the dead. Such tablets, whose shape resembles the early mastabas, were often erected at Abydos, the funerary cult centre of Osiris, even after its abandonment as the actual burial ground. Eighteenth Dynasty. Museo Archeologico, Florence.

Below left. The Fourth-Dynasty pyramid of Khephren at Giza, almost 450 feet high and made of limestone from the cliffs lining the Nile Valley. Elaborate tombs of the pharaohs, the pyramids were built partly by slave labour and partly by agricultural workers in the season of the Nile floods.

Below right. Pectoral with falcon, vulture and *uraeus* motifs flanked by *djed*-columns symbolic of Osiris. The amulet thus combines the protective power of four major dynastic deities, from Upper, Lower and Middle Egypt. Musée du Louvre, Paris.

would have seemed quite irrelevant.

The merging of the various gods may have been facilitated also by similarities between them based on their roots in the same agricultural and geographical setting; but that the gods never quite coalesced, giving up their original features, may be due to the fact that to the ancient Egyptians it was ritual that was the fount of belief. Divine rites were re-enactments of the processes of nature and agriculture and of the social order. As among all agricultural peoples, such rites in their primitive forms were intended to ensure that nature should indeed be beneficent. In the case of Egypt, with the favourable conditions along the Nile, the rites were perhaps more celebratory than based on fear.

Ritual changes slowly and reluctantly, but the condition of the worshippers may alter rapidly, especially so far as the social order is concerned. Myths are the means by which they are able to relate the traditional ritual to their actual circumstances and to the introduction of new gods and new cults.

We are beginning to learn more about the nature of Egyptian religion. The artistic representations of religious subjects, most of which became fixed at a relatively early stage, perhaps in the Second Dynasty, are in general more concerned with the cult or ritual than with the depiction of mythological stories. The emphasis on ritual is the reason for some of our difficulty in understanding Egypt's

Above. Apis, the bull representing the composite god of creation, the necropolis, and hopes of rebirth, Ptah-Seker-Osiris. As a detail from the coffin of Denytenamon, a Twentieth-Dynasty priest of Amon-Ra at Thebes, it not only illustrates the coalescence and propitiation of disparate gods, but also the importance of the priesthood, for in earliest times hopes of rebirth to eternal life and the accompanying mortuary rites were restricted to royalty. British Museum, London.

Opposite. Woman worshipping the goddess Hathor and presenting her with offerings in the form of food. New Kingdom period, c. 1300 B.C.

religion – and also much other primitive belief. Though all-embracing and dominating every aspect of the individual's life, the ancient Egyptian religion was not fixed and static in a dogmatic creed, as the ritual would suggest. It was rather a creative religion where every believer was called on to use his imagination. Each enactment of ritual was not only a reminder of some myth concerned with the gods, it also *was* those events. On the other hand, any deviation from the accustomed ritual, for

whatever reason, could entail a revision of the myth. This, as well as the many centuries of change during which the Egyptian religion prevailed, may account for the inconsistencies which are apparent between the various sources of our knowledge of the religion: the carvings and statuary of the temples and the mural paintings in tombs and illustrated papyri, or manuscripts. There is some reason to believe that the ancient Egyptians might have regarded what we would term inconsistencies as something like

the differences between two poems interpreting the same theme; each had its own justification in the imagination of its author. In general, too, and for reasons which will become apparent, educated Egyptians grew to regard their gods as mere symbols of cosmic or ethical forces. In the sophisticated times of the New Kingdom (1570-1085 B.C.), when many religious benefits formerly reserved for the pharaoh or for the nobility had been extended to the whole people, myths seem at times to have become so detached from faith as to be treated as entertainment. The peasants may have taken the symbols literally, but we know little of their beliefs. Despite the artistic representation of the gods and other evidence, modern scholars increasingly reject the view that the Egyptians worshipped animals themselves as gods; rather they worshipped the qualities with which they imagined these

animals to be especially endowed.

The earliest tribal gods may have been fetishes connected with nomadic hunting or warrior peoples. But most of these tribes settled at some stage in prehistory; their gods became local gods and were associated with agriculture. Early mythology therefore explained them in terms of earth and water, rain and sky. One of the commonest of the tribal fetishes was the falcon, which soon became identified with the sky, perhaps simply because the falcon was able to fly so high. The most powerful of these falcon-deities was Horus, whose people probably came from Libya and apparently conquered large parts of Upper and Lower Egypt. At an early period many falcon-gods seem to have been merged with Horus, but not, apparently, as the result of an organised conquest. Horus peoples were living unconnected with each other in different parts of the Nile valley, and as

peaceful neighbours beside the followers of other early deities – both local town gods and those which had achieved a certain universality, such as Isis, Osiris and Set. Despite the indigenous belief that the sun was a force of destruction and the enemy of the farmer, the Horus peoples also lived in peace beside the followers of a sun-god, Ra, who probably came from the islands of the Mediterranean, or perhaps from the Caucasus.

Much emphasis is placed in Egyptian writings on the 'Two Lands', Upper and Lower Egypt, and with reason: though they had a natural tendency to separate, often demonstrated in history, their unification was always a prerequisite for the development of Egyptian civilisation. The first unification seems to have been achieved by followers of Ra, who set up their capital at Heliopolis, which was to remain the chief theological and academic centre of Egypt over many dynasties. Though this prehistoric political supremacy of the followers of Ra was shortlived, the fact that their ruler was the first to achieve Egyptian unification had lasting consequences: it permanently associated the concept of supreme rule with sun cults. Force of tradition thereafter required that every major god, and particularly those of the pharaohs, should be connected with or identified with the sun. It also meant that when other gods achieved greater popular following there were distinct differences between the official gods of the kingdom and those of the people.

The first important coalescence of hitherto incompatible gods occurred about 3100 B.C. under Menes or Narmer, the founder of the First Dynasty and the first king of whom we have historical records. Menes was a follower of Horus, the falcon-god, and king of one of the branches of the followers of Horus which had settled in Upper Egypt, and had become supreme there. Menes established his first capital of a united Egypt at Thinis, on the borders between Upper and Lower Egypt and near Abydos, the holy city of the fertility-god

Osiris, whose cult and popularity had already spread peacefully throughout Egypt. Menes subsequently built Memphis, the 'White Walls', as his imperial city, on a site quite close to the centre of the sun cult, Heliopolis. Horus the sky-god henceforth had earthly connections with the sun cult and with fertility cults. As we shall see, it was only a matter of time before mythology connected the gods Horus, Ra and Osiris.

In these early dynastic times the pattern for all future pharaohs was being laid down. It was considered that the pharaoh was divinely appointed to rule, to be the intermediary between his people and the gods; and his nature and those of the gods were closely identified. Delegated to rule by the gods, the pharaoh was soon thought to be descended from them and to partake of their divine nature. This development was reinforced by the position of the king as intermediary and, in theory, the only officiant allowed to approach the gods as their priest. In the cult the gods were treated as if they were kings on earth; the main features of the ritual being an elaborate toilet, in which the god was anointed and

decked with jewels, given a symbolic meal and entertained with occasional processions among the people, often by boat, during which he might be called upon to give judgement in some matter of concern to the worshippers. This might well involve the settlement of a dispute over land tenure or taxes in kind of the sort which in earthly terms were the jurisdiction of the pharaoh. As the gods were like kings on earth, so the pharaohs came to be considered godlike. They had both earthly power over the lives of their subjects and, as priests, apparently had spiritual power over the forces of nature.

The early Horus-kings may have been associated with the sky-god as rainmakers, but they were also dispensers of discipline or justice, and in this aspect they could easily be identified with cosmic gods – particularly the sun, Ra – whose regular courses were symbolic of divine order and justice, personified by the goddess Mayet. There was a reverse side to the benefits conferred by the Nile and by the sun: the Nile floods could and often did fail; the sun was visibly a destructive as well as a creative force. The surrounding desert, which gave

Opposite left. A bronze statue of Bast, the benevolent cat-goddess of Bubastis. Animals and birds were widely revered in ancient Egypt, usually as representatives of the species associated with a major deity. Frequently the cult was local, and often a creature held sacred in one city was regarded elsewhere as the enemy of mankind. c. 1000 B.C.

Opposite right. The victory palette of Narmer, the southern chieftain who established the first stable unification of North and South. He is seen wearing the white crown of Upper Egypt and brandishing a mace over a captive. The Horus falcon, whose follower he was, tramples underfoot six Delta plants, each symbolic of a thousand Lower Egyptian captives. He leads their chieftain by the nose. First Dynasty, from Hierakonpolis. Egyptian Museum, Cairo.

Right. The ancient Egyptian believed that his gods shared his own material needs. Offerings of food, drink and riches were therefore an important part of the cult. This bearer carries lotus flowers and jars containing libations (usually of beer, milk, oil or wine). Musée du Louvre, Paris.

Top. The deceased and his wife paddling boats in the happy afterlife, a fertile land provided with ample watercourses, never far from the Nile. Below, the deceased ploughs and reaps the fields of Osiris in the afterworld where, as in the land of the living, communal effort ensured prosperity for the land. Detail from the *Book of the Dead.* Twentieth-Dynasty Papyrus of Oneru. Museo Egizio, Turin.

Above. Head of Seti I from a relief in the temple of Abydos. He is receiving the *sa ankh*, the symbol of life-essence transferred from the 'great god' to the pharaoh or 'good god' during the daily temple ritual. Having received this, the pharaoh could perform his ritual duties towards the god, from which acts he derived his power. Nineteenth Dynasty.

Opposite. A painting from the tomb of Horemheb (1348–1320 B.C.) showing him on the left facing Osiris and in the centre offering wine to Ament, goddess of the West, whose hawk emblem is on her head. Originally goddess of a Libyan province to the west of Egypt, Ament was identified with Hathor as goddess of the Underworld when 'West' came to signify land of the dead. Late Eighteenth Dynasty.

Egypt physical unity and protected it from easy invasion, was also a constant reminder to the valley inhabitants of their special dependence on the beneficent influence of nature. The king, as representative and priest of the gods of the Nile and of the sun, had to be placated. He was the upholder of the divine order: what he willed was good; what was unforeseen or accepted unwillingly, such as natural disasters, was evil. Prosperity and generally favourable conditions led to the insistence on maintaining the status quo and led also to the wish to maintain it in the afterlife and so to the apparent preoccupation with death already mentioned. An even,

regular pattern of agriculture was the greatest good, so that in the afterlife all were occupied in farming just as they were in good years on earth, when levies obliged all men to work in the fields. (This was the theory: actually in life rich men supplied servants as substitutes and in death they were furnished with *ushabti* figures which would perform manual work for them in the afterlife.)

Just as the Egyptians made little distinction between cult and theology, so the boundaries between religion and what we should nowadays call politics were ill-defined. In so far as Church and State can be distinguished in ancient Egypt, it is

clear that each supported the other. The king was regarded as divine, and in later times may actually have been accorded worship as a god during his lifetime – though there is some dispute on this among scholars, who point out that the pharaoh was referred to as 'good god', whereas the gods whom he represented on earth were referred to as 'great gods'. But whether a god himself or not, the pharaoh's rule on earth amounted to a ritual re-enactment of mythological events.

A large part of mythology as we know it was concerned therefore with the setting up of a hierarchy on earth, with a system of land tenure and with

the establishment of ritual forms. Egyptian mythology can be interpreted as an attempt to bolster up the authority of the king, and certainly some changes in religious belief can be traced to the opening of a new dynasty or a shift of power from one part of the country to another. This, however, is an essentially modern view of the situation. The ancient Egyptian really believed that his king had divine authority, not merely that he claimed it as a justification for his rule. He believed that the king was the direct intermediary between the gods and men, and that without the king the divine benefits could not be extended to the ordinary inhabitants of the country. The king's actions and his welfare were therefore of prime importance to every one of his subjects. The king in his turn owed scrupulous devotion to the gods and by fulfilling his daily ritual duties constantly renewed his own divine nature.

As we shall see, the welfare of the pharaoh's soul after death was of equal if not of greater importance, this being one of the ways in which the state religion absorbed the popular Osiris cult. To this fact we owe the most complete literature we have on the Egyptian religion in its basic and most vigorous phase. The *Pyramid Texts*, a collection of spells and incantations whose purpose was to ensure the safe passage of the pharaohs to the next world and their divine transfiguration, give us the best clues to the beliefs alluded to in the mythological scenes of art. Apart from this, full-length narrative or drama based on the myths survives only from a fairly late period. The *Pyramid Texts*, however, rank among the oldest known religious literature in the world, the earliest texts dating from about the middle of the third millennium B.C., when they were preserved in the royal pyramids of the Fifth and the Sixth Dynasties. Democratisation of the burial customs once reserved for the pharaoh alone, the belief in times of royal weakness that ordinary mortals might be justified by works and could aspire to an afterlife, inevitably had its effect on

the mythology; but the *Coffin Texts* and the *Book of the Dead*, which were the successors to the *Pyramid Texts* in the Twelfth and Thirteenth Dynasties, were relatively little adapted to the new beliefs. They too, therefore, can tell us much about the earlier forms of myth and can help to explain the pictorial and ritual representation of the gods with their attendant recurring symbols, both equally frozen in their early styles.

Though the antecedents of the Egyptian gods may have been tribal fetishes of hunting peoples; though in the conservative Egyptian fashion they may never have shaken off some of the attributes of the original deity; and though in particular they retained their appearance in art, many being represented as animals, or with animal heads, or perhaps simply with horns – nevertheless the Egyptian gods were early anthropomorphised. The nature of the cult, the interaction of reality and myth and the identification of the pharaoh with the falcon-god Horus all underline this fact. The gods looked somewhat like their early followers – warriors wearing a short 'kilt'. They wore stylised 'Puntite' beards, plaited and curved, thought to be symbolic of a goat as embodiment of fertility; behind them hung a bushy animal's tail. Throughout historic times the pharaohs wore kilt and tail, and the priests too, especially during the New Kingdom, wore archaic costume. The goddesses wore simple ankle-length dresses. The heavy wigs which both gods and goddesses wore softened the transition from their animal heads to their human shoulders. The early fetish, where it was not an animal, was often incorporated as an attribute carried in the hand or on the head, or in the accompanying hieroglyph for the deity's name. Such were the thunderbolt of Min or the crossed arrows of Neith.

As we have remarked, the cult devoted to these gods was officially the prerogative and duty of the pharaoh alone, and the conscientious fulfilment of this duty was of vital importance to the people and to him. The cults reflected the contemporary

established social order, and at the same time they served to justify it. In this sense their function was similar to that of primitive magic, where the depiction of a situation in ritual images or, still more strongly, the ritual declamation of it would make the events in question actually occur or would give a situation the force of law. While the pharaoh himself might actually perform the most important ceremonies of the year, he clearly could not officiate every day at every temple in the land. In each sanctuary therefore the king was represented by a high priest.

Originally these high priests were important men in the cult city specially honoured by the king through being selected and often endowed by him with land and wealth. In time it became the custom in many places, notably Thebes, the cult centre of Amon-Ra, to make the office of high priest hereditary, so that the priests acquired independent standing and power. Many of their duties were in turn delegated to full-time scribes and lay officiants who took turns in performing the temple ritual, each serving for one of the four watches in the daily cycle. Priestesses also served in the temples, usually dancing and making music in the forecourt for the entertainment of the god. The priestesses were deemed to be the god's concubines in the temples of gods associated with fertility, especially those of Amon-Ra, where the Divine Consort was often a royal princess. The high priest's assistants acted as a sort of bureaucracy with responsibility for the god's domains. Indirectly they also acted as judges and administrators. When the god was borne forth into the city, held aloft in his golden boat (his progress thus imitating that of the pharaoh along the Nile when he inspected his domains) petitions in the form of contradictory propositions would be put to him. The case was judged according to whether the god, borne by the priests, advanced or retreated. This practice was at odds with the usual belief that the extent to which a god had been pleased by his people was shown only in their degree of prosperity.

The position of the high priest was therefore in many ways parallel to that of the pharaoh and, like the monarchs or provincial governors, he gained in power whenever the royal authority was weakened – as it was at times of military defeat or when the pharaonic blood was mixed with that of commoners and ordinary mortals. This trend was at its height during the New Kingdom and in the Late Period, when the god Amon-Ra rose to supremacy. Wealth gained by conquest poured into the coffers of the priesthood of Amon-Ra, and further wealth was expended on the cult. The economy was weakened and the royal house with it, while the priests of Amon-Ra consolidated their power

and endowments. The high priest of Amon-Ra ruled the priests of all the other cults, and himself became a kingmaker in the Eighteenth Dynasty, supporting Hatshepsut, the first woman to reign as pharaoh, and her successor Thuthmosis III. Though overthrown by Akhenaten, Amon-Ra made a quick recovery after the heretical pharaoh's death, and three centuries later his high priest claimed the overlordship of Upper Egypt for king Amon-Ra himself, his rule to be exercised through the priesthood.

The Twenty-first Dynasty, which maintained close rule over the North and nominal rule over the South, was in practice ineffective in Upper Egypt, and thus initiated the beginning of

Above. Pharaoh, honoured as a god by men, was himself obliged to honour the gods. In this granite carving of the Nineteenth Dynasty Rameses II kneels to make an offering. Musée du Louvre, Paris.

Below left. The terrace temple of Queen Hatshepsut, built at Deir el Bahri in the Theban necropolis at the side of an Eleventh-Dynasty mortuary temple. Unlike the other royal tombs of the Eighteenth Dynasty, which were hewn out of the rock face in the remote Valley of the Kings and were separate from the mortuary temples of the Nile valley, Hatshepsut's tomb was connected to her temple by a long causeway.

Below right. Section of a symbolic tableau of the course of the sun. Four minor divinities with scarab and serpent heads bear Ra-Harakhte, the sun-god, in triumph. New Kingdom period, c. 1300 B.C. Bibliothèque Nationale, Paris.

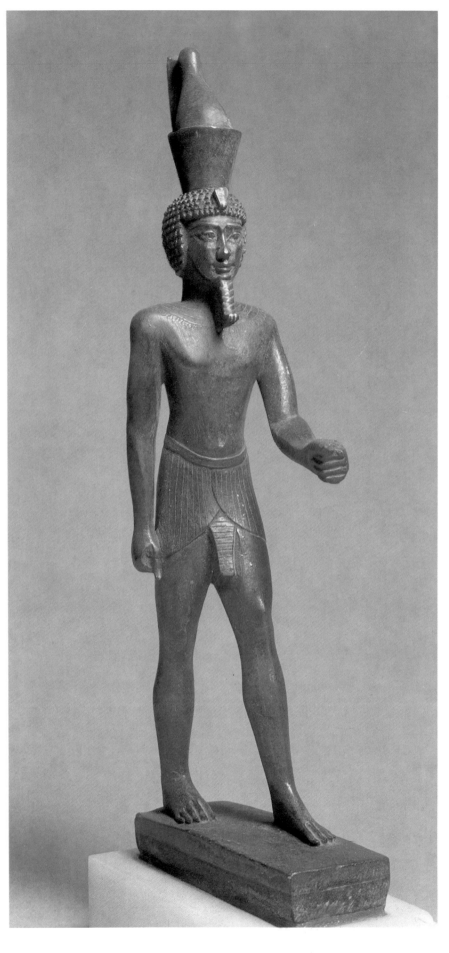

ancient Egypt's long decline. But the priesthood too was weakened by this change in the established order, for the high priest who thus established semi-independence was influenced by members of a military family which had infiltrated the priesthood of Amon-Ra. Subsequently the pharaoh ensured the goodwill of the Amon-Ra priesthood by making his own son high priest, and so breaking the dynastic tradition of inherited priestly office. Thus though the priests officially were the representatives of the pharaoh, owed their position to him, and ostensibly supported him, they could wield the power vested in them in unexpected ways. These developments, however, were far distant at the time when the early Egyptian faith was being evolved and elaborated, when mythology sought to explain the forces of nature as observed by a simple, orderly, agricultural people.

By and large, during the period when Egypt was a unified country, all the important gods which had formerly been local divinities were worshipped throughout the land. Special prominence may have been given to a particular god in the city or region of that god's provenance, but he was in general related in some mythological scheme to the other gods worshipped in the remainder of Egypt.

Basically, the most prominent of the gods throughout the history of ancient Egypt in some way represented the powers of creation, of fertility or of the sun. Even the ancient cult of Osiris, which dominated Egyptian religion in later times, was gradually changed from a cult of the dead to a cult of fertility or of life, even if this was life after death. As we shall see, Osiris became increasingly identified with the sun and gradually entered the realm of the living. The association of the cult of the dead with fertility cults was, of course, not unique to Egypt. It occurs again and again, notably in the Greek myth of Hades and Persephone. This may be why the myth of Osiris particularly interested Plutarch when he visited Egypt. The Osiris myth cycle is one of the few that has been transmitted to us in any detail (with considerable

accuracy, archaeological evidence shows), and it is to Plutarch that we owe this. Death was not unknown to the gods themselves, particularly the early Lords of the City.

The god Horus, symbolised by a falcon, was in the beginning an exception to the general rule that the chief gods were associated with fertility or creation. As we have remarked, he was originally the god of a hunting people, or possibly a war-god, but after the unification of Egypt by Menes he began to be identified with the sun cult of a king who had earlier unified the Two Lands. The falcon became the symbol of majesty and the archetype of the pharaohs, who were said to be seated on his throne. Attempts to incorporate worship of the sun into the Horus legend took the form of making the divine falcon a sky-god, the sun being his right eye and the moon his left eye.

As a sky-god, Horus could equally take his part in the body of myth connected with agriculture. Water, to the Egyptians, was the source of fertility, and the sky was considered to be an ocean mirroring that on earth from which the Nile took its source. The heavenly bodies also played their part in agriculture; for example the Dog-star, called Septet or Sothis and later identified with Isis, rose with the sun in the eastern sky at the exact time of year when the Nile floods were due to inaugurate the new agricultural year, and was venerated accordingly. Study of the heavens was intense at Heliopolis, and the connections between astronomy and the phases of agriculture were soon discovered.

The identification of Horus with the sun became still closer in the Fifth Dynasty, when Heliopolis and its cult of the sun-god Ra regained its religious supremacy. Horus now became the son of Ra. In later times this falcon-Horus was confused with another god called Horus, who was the son of Isis and Osiris or the son of Geb and Nut and therefore the grandson of the sun-god. The composite god which emerged from this confusion retained the falcon symbol and the associations with majesty and power, but he also figured in the afterlife myths of Osiris. On the other hand, his association with the Osiris myth helps to explain how Osiris gradually left the realm of the dead and entered that of the living, and both gods had important roles in the interplay of myth and ritual concerning the living and the dead which increasingly dominated the Egyptian religion. It seems unlikely that Osiris and the cult of the dead or ancestor worship would have attained such importance if the two Horus gods had not been amalgamated.

Though in this sense there is continuity or perhaps a cyclic pattern in the formulation of Egyptian beliefs, religious systems were by no means left to evolve naturally in the minds of the people at large. It would be wrong to over-emphasise the deliberate changing of doctrine by kings or by priests to suit their own ambitions, but it is impossible to understand such knowledge as we have of beliefs held about the various gods without some consideration of the basic systems of the great cult centres.

Contemporary evidence of the beliefs of the Egyptians is contained in religious documents produced in the cult centres. These documents are couched in the symbolic language of ritual based on mythological events as understood in each centre. We are thus able to guess at the underlying systems by examining the implications of the ritual embodied in the texts. Before we discuss each individual god, it is necessary to consider the doctrines of the four great cult centres, Heliopolis, Hermopolis, Memphis and Thebes. The cult of Osiris, which in its earlier forms pre-dated and in its later forms gradually supplanted these systems, will be discussed separately.

The body of myths, many of which are common to the whole of Egypt and to all historical ages, covers the period from the creation of the world to the rise of Horus as king. From that time on, Horus was to be ritually represented on earth by each successive pharaoh, whose rise to power was identified with that of Horus. Of the trials of Horus before he became king we have a fairly full record, for his cult became bound up with that of Osiris and was therefore still of considerable importance when Egypt began to come into contact with the

Adoration of Ra at his rising in the east by seven figures of Thoth. Below is the *djed*-column, which represents Osiris, worshipped by Isis and Nephthys. Theban *Book of the Dead*, from the Papyrus of Hunefer. Early Nineteenth Dynasty. British Museum, London.

outside world and with such observers as Herodotus and Plutarch. Of the earlier part of the myth sequence we have less certain knowledge. But doctrinal differences between the four great cult centres hinged on their differing interpretations of the creation of the world. As the pharaoh exercised his power by virtue of heredity and his divine birth, so the gods owed their position to their mythological origin. Their power was justified by their origin and function in the cosmogony. Hence the importance of the cosmogonies attaching to the various political centres and the fusion and subjugation of one to the other for mythological development.

It seems more accurate to call the varying systems different interpretations rather than different beliefs, for the cults were generally regarded, certainly by the educated, as being aspects of the same truths. Apparently, except during the brief period of Atenism, the only priests who were at all dogmatic were those of Heliopolis, and their cult is the most completely known to us. The other systems were essentially variants of the Heliopolitan doctrine, and made little attempt to reconcile all the inconsistencies resulting from superimposition of one cult on another. The Egyptians may well have thought that a succession of fleeting images, a symbol language or notation for spiritual ideas, gave a better picture of the essentially unknowable.

This was largely the technique even of the religious texts produced in the four great cult centres when expounding that part of their doctrine – the cosmogony – in which they specifically needed to make themselves clear in order to set themselves apart from their rivals. Instead, the priests of each cult centre seem to have borrowed aspects of their rivals' doctrine – perhaps in an attempt to be all-inclusive.

The Creation of the World

All Egyptian cosmogonies were basically concerned with divinities of nature: the sky, the earth, the wind, the sun, the moon and the stars. The other gods which figured in the cosmogonies were possibly not originally connected with the creation legends, but were grafted on to the systems because of ethical or political considerations. As the priesthood was identified with the solar kingship, the cosmogonies were designed to incorporate the sun and other cosmic forces into the popular cult systems based on local and fertility deities. Many local gods became solarised, but each contributed his own elements to the solar mythology. In the Heliopolitan system all the forms which the sun thus acquired were combined.

The Egyptians imagined the sky to be a goddess. She was pictured as a cow standing over the earth, supported by other deities, with the barque of the sun sailing along her starry belly, which was a heavenly ocean; or as an elongated woman bending over the earth and held up by the god of wind or air, Shu, or by the chain of high mountains bounding the earth. Beneath her lay the circular ocean, in the centre of which was Geb, the earth-god, lying prone with vegetation sprouting from his back. Part of the earth was red, and inhabited by the barbarians of the desert, and part was black, the fertile lands of the Nile valley. The waters of the ocean or the Nile flowed also into an Underworld, abode of the dead, which was a mirror of the heavens and through which the night-barque of the sun sailed.

The sun, most important of the Egyptian deities, had many names, and the interpretations given to his functions were extremely varied. As a sun-disk he was called Aten; as the rising sun his name was Khepri, a great scarab beetle rolling before him the globe of the sun, just as on earth the scarab rolls before it a ball of dung in which it has laid its eggs and from which will burst forth life; as the sun climbed to his zenith he was called Ra, supreme god of Heliopolis; and as he set as an old man he was called Atum. He was also called Horus, and when this aspect was combined with that of Ra as Ra-Harakhte he was seen as the youthful sun of the horizon, a winged sun-disk. He was said to be born every morning as a golden calf from the heavenly cow, or to be swallowed every night by the celestial woman and reborn daily from her. Sometimes he was thought not to be sailing perpetually on the oceans of heaven or the Underworld, but to reside on an island in the heavenly ocean, in whose waters he bathed each morning; or to live on the horizon, or in the fields of the blessed. He was also said to be an egg laid daily by the 'Great Cackler' – Geb, the earth, in the form of a water-fowl – or a falcon with speckled wings flying through space, or the right eye of the falcon – the left eye being the moon.

The moon was also said to be the sun's brother and son of Nut, the sky. He was sometimes identified with Osiris and at other times with the god of learning, Thoth, when he was represented as an ibis or as a dog-headed baboon. His other forms were as Aah and Khonsu.

The stars were children of the sky-goddess as a sow, who gave birth to them in the morning and swallowed them at night. Alternatively

they were the souls of the dead and served as courtiers to the sun-king Ra. The morning star attended the sun, bringing him breakfast and washing his face every morning.

The ancient Egyptians imagined that in the beginning the universe was filled with a primordial ocean called Nun. Though sometimes compared to a great waste of floodwaters and no doubt inspired by the Nile inundations, Nun had no surface: it completely filled the universe and could be likened to a cosmic egg. The waters of Nun were motionless, or stagnant. We do not know whether the Egyptians necessarily considered Nun to be potentially or inevitably life-bearing; certainly if we are to pursue the analogy with the Nile floodwaters, we can see that the Egyptians would have witnessed the apparently miraculous way in which as the waters subside the pools they leave behind soon swarm with animal life. But we are given no clear indication of what the Egyptians thought had started the creative process: if it was immanent in Nun, which was featureless and eternal, why did creation in fact happen at a particular moment in the eternity of time?

Another notion accepted in all the

cosmogonies was that of the primeval hill rising out of Nun. The priests of each of the four great cult centres claimed that their temple stood on the site of this primeval hill; probably the first to make this claim were the Heliopolitans, but for their own prestige the other temples had to claim the same privilege for themselves. The first pyramids were doubtless symbolic representations of the primeval mound, and also resembled the steps on the banks of the Nile used to measure the height of the fertilising flood. It was sometimes imagined that, like the land emerging from the Nile floodwaters and eventually being inundated by them again, so the earth which had emerged from Nun might one day again be swallowed up into the primordial waste of waters.

Whatever details the Egyptians may have ascribed to the events and sequence of creation – and they tended to regard it as a slow development rather than as an instantaneous act of creation – they shared the view that what they called the 'First Time', or the age in which gods actually lived on earth and had their kingdoms there, was a golden age in which the principles of justice reigned over the land. Provided the successor

Above. Shu, god of the atmosphere, raising his daughter Nut away from Geb and thus creating the world. He is aided by two ram-deities – associated with creation. Top left, the bull and Eye of Ra, whose daily course was along Nut's body and who was said to be born of her anew each day. Painted coffin of Butehamon. Museo di Antichità, Turin.

Opposite above. Shu, god of the air, supporting the Barque of Millions of Years with its crew of the great gods of the First Time, in which the sun traversed the heavens by day and the Underworld by night. The sun is seen as Khepri, the scarab beetle that symbolised the rising sun, and the disk is received by the sky-goddess Nut. In the centre a mummy lies on a bier shaped like the primeval mound amidst the waters of the cosmic ocean Nun, awaiting rebirth. *Book of the Dead.* Papyrus of Anhai, seen on the right, a priestess of Amon-Ra. Twentieth Dynasty, c. 1100 B.C. British Museum, London.

Opposite below. The Step Pyramid at Saqqara, built by the Third-Dynasty pharaoh Djoser as his tomb.

to these gods, the pharaoh, could maintain the sway of justice, Mayet – and theology was designed to support him in this task – the actual conditions in Egypt could be likened to those of the golden age and Egyptians could accept their appointed place and their role in maintaining the pharaoh's strength.

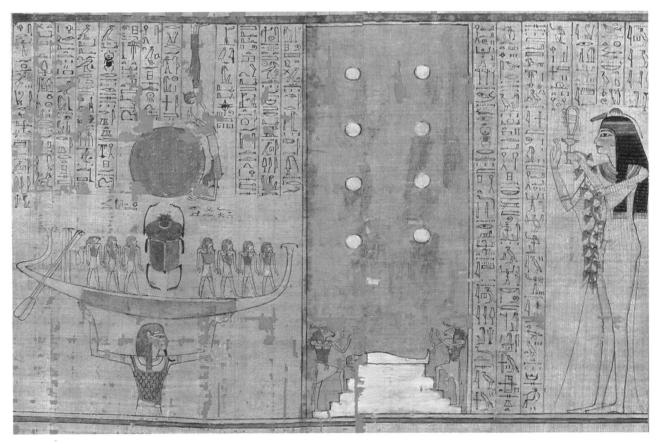

Below. A limestone relief of the early Fifth Dynasty representing the god of the waters – probably Atmu, or the bisexual Atum, who emerged from the waters of Nun to form the primeval hill and then the deities Shu and Tefnut.

Opposite. Pectoral, one of many designed to be attached to specified points on the mummified bodies of the dead. It shows the divine mourners Isis and Nephthys supporting a scarab, symbol of renewed life, whose inclusion in the tomb was intended to ensure the rebirth of the deceased in the afterlife. Musée du Louvre, Paris.

The Heliopolitan Cosmogony

Though the Heliopolitan priests seem to have been the most doctrinaire, we have no clear exposition of their beliefs. The greatest religious document which has survived from Heliopolis, the Fifth-Dynasty *Pyramid Texts*, makes only passing references to creation, assuming basic knowledge of Heliopolitan doctrine.

It seems that in this the first event in the creative process was the emergence of Atum, the god of Heliopolis, from the chaotic wastes of Nun. Atum created himself by an effort of will; or he was the child of Nun. Finding nowhere to stand, he created at the place of his first appearance a hill which was later to be surmounted by the temple of Heliopolis. According to other, earlier interpretations, Atum, whose name meant something like the 'completed one', thus connecting him with creation, was himself the hill. Atum would then resemble the life-engendering hillocks left behind by the receding waters of the Nile. But as Atum had by the time of the *Pyramid Texts* become identified with the sun god Ra, his emergence on the primeval hill was also interpreted as the coming of light to disperse the chaotic darkness of Nun. In this aspect Ra-Atum was symbolised by the Bennu bird or phoenix, which alighted at dawn on the Benben, an obelisk representing a ray of the sun. In another aspect, Ra-Atum was symbolised by the scarab beetle pushing his egg out in front of him, thus starting with his appearance the new cycle of creation. His name in this aspect was Khepri, 'He who comes into existence', later fixed as a symbol for the rising sun.

Atum was 'He who created himself'. His next act was to create further gods. As he was alone in the world, he had to produce offspring without a mate. His means was union with his shadow, or masturbation. This did not in any way appear to shock the Egyptians. Atum seems often in the texts to be regarded as a

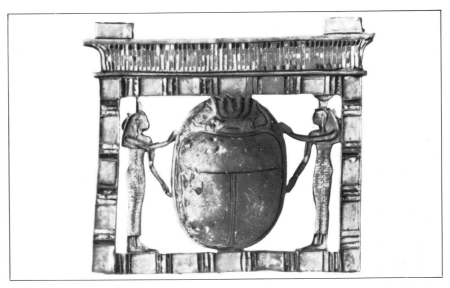

bisexual god and was sometimes called the 'Great He-She'. Conceiving of creation only in terms of sexual generation, the Egyptians were able through this episode in the myth to present Atum as an intensely powerful creative force owing nothing to the agency of another.

Atum gave birth to his son Shu by spitting him out, and to his daughter Tefnut by vomiting her forth. Shu's function as god of the air sprang naturally from the form of his birth; Tefnut seems to have had little significance in the Heliopolitan cosmogony except as consort of Shu. But the priests' interpretations even at a fairly early date made Shu the life principle and Tefnut the principle of world order – called Mayet, the name of a generally distinct goddess. Shu and Tefnut thus became suitable deities to carry on the creative cycle and establish a social order. Where these early events took place is uncertain. According to some texts Shu and Tefnut were created on the primeval hill. According to others, Atum remained in the waters of Nun and there created his son and daughter; Shu and Tefnut were brought up by Nun and looked after by Atum's Eye.

Atum seems only to have had one eye and it was physically separable from him and independent in its wishes. Two important myths relate to this Eye, the *udjat*. In the first Shu and Tefnut, who were still under Atum's protection, became separated from him in the dark wastes of the

waters of Nun. Atum sent his Eye to look for them and eventually Shu and Tefnut came back with the Eye. While the Eye had been searching for Shu and Tefnut, Atum had replaced it with another, and much brighter one. The first Eye was enraged with Atum at finding itself supplanted when it returned. Atum therefore took the first Eye and placed it on his forehead where it could rule the whole world which he was about to create. The Eye was often depicted as a destructive goddess – one aspect of the burning sun in Egypt, and it was associated with the cobra-goddess, Buto or Edjo, the rearing serpent which was in fact shown in the form of the *uraeus* on the foreheads of the pharaohs, as a symbolic representation of their power.

When Atum was reunited with Shu and Tefnut he wept for joy, and from his tears grew men. With the return of his children, Atum was ready to leave the waters of Nun and to create the world.

Shu and Tefnut became the parents of Geb, the earth, and his sister and wife Nut, the sky. With their birth, the divinities of the major aspects of nature were all accounted for. Geb and Nut were, however, the parents of four children who had no such cosmic associations. They were Isis and Osiris, Nephthys and Set. Horus, archetype of the pharaohs, was the son of Isis and Osiris, or was sometimes called the son of Nut. It may be that these deities were incorporated

into the basic Heliopolitan cosmogony by the priests, who wished to subordinate them to their own original gods. However that may be, this so-called Ennead of Heliopolis was a well-established tradition in the Egyptian religion, and the same family relationships were described in the literature of the other cult centres. Perhaps other cults were also incorporated but incompletely assimilated by the Heliopolitan priests, for other inconsistencies occur in their texts. An example is the confusion over the origin of Atum: generally he was considered to be self created, but he was sometimes called the child of Nun, and this may be accounted for by an attempt of the theologians to subordinate Atum to another legend which

attributed the work of creation to Nun (perhaps in this situation identified with the Nile).

Similarly some texts said that Horus was the son of Geb and Nut, and that he and his four brothers and sisters were together responsible for the procreation of the 'multitudes in the land'; whereas in other texts, Nut was called 'mother of the gods' and also 'she who bears Ra each day'. Atum was even described as setting Geb over the Ennead, which included himself. Indeed, the priests of Heliopolis considered themselves to be the representatives on earth of Geb and Nut, rather than of their chief god Atum. Again, in the *Pyramid Texts*, the pharaoh Pepi is declared in one passage to have been engendered by

Above. The Eye of Atum, which was separable from him and which he placed on his brow where it could rule the world. Known as the *udjat*, it was a mystic emblem of royal power, here seen flanked by the vulture and cobra goddesses of Upper and Lower Egypt, Nekhebet and Edjo or Buto. On the royal crown it was Edjo who represented the Eye as the *uraeus*. The Eye entered the mythology of Ra when Ra and Atum coalesced. Pectoral of the pharaoh Tutankhamon and found in the innermost mummy wrappings, suggesting that it was worn during his lifetime. Eighteenth Dynasty. Egyptian Museum, Cairo.

Opposite. Sesostris I embraced by Ptah of Memphis. Though Ptah was not considered the mightiest of the gods outside Memphis, he and his city, founded as the 'White Walls' by the first pharaoh, Menes, remained central in the coronation of kings and the *sed*-festivals in which their authority was renewed. Detail from a pillar.

Atum before the creation of the earth, the heavens, men, gods and death; and in another passage he seems to be called the son of Nun: 'born in Nun before the creation of the heavens, earth, and the disorder and fear brought by the eye of Horus'. This hyperbole may of course not reflect the true Heliopolitan doctrine, but may merely be a poetic image or kind of magic incantation designed to ensure the safe passage of the king's soul to the afterworld by asserting his divine origin. For such was the purpose of the texts which have survived to us, rather than that of the reasoned exposition of any specific religious doctrine.

The Memphite Cosmogony

At the opening of the historical period, about 3000 B.C., Upper and Lower Egypt were joined by the pharaoh Menes. He built a new capital for the united country near the apex of the Nile delta. The city, Memphis, was known as the 'White Walls'. Older cities, such as Heliopolis, were not far distant, and no doubt it seemed particularly important to the early rulers to assert the superiority of the new city, not merely as the seat of the centralised government and thus of prime political importance, but also as a religious centre superior to all others in the land. The political background goes a long way towards explaining the particular form taken by the cosmogony of Memphis.

Ptah, the high god of Memphis and god as the master of destiny, was declared to be the creator of the world. The whole Heliopolitan cosmogony was not thereby set aside entirely, but it was claimed that the deities of the Heliopolitan Ennead were merely manifestations of the supreme god Ptah. The Shabaka Stone, a late copy of an early text, which is the source of our knowledge of Memphite theology, is very clear on this point. The tone of the Shabaka Stone text is polemical: it seems to take each point of the Heliopolitan beliefs in order almost to turn it upside down. This reinforces our belief that the priests

of Memphis were concerned, for the glory of their own city, to deny a more widely held view of creation.

The Shabaka Stone declared that Ptah was he who sat upon the Great Throne: he was therefore identified with the Great God who, like the Great Mother, was early worshipped in Egypt, perhaps as a fertility-deity. Ptah was then declared to be Nun, the Father, who begot Atum and also Naunet (the female form of Nun), the Mother, who bore Atum. The text went on to say that Ptah was the Heart and the Tongue of the Ennead (i.e. of Heliopolis). The heart and the tongue were generally considered by the Egyptians to be respectively the seats of the mind or intelligence and of command or power; they were therefore regarded as symbols of Atum, the creator. In the Memphite system Atum was thus merely the agent of Ptah's will, who understood his commands and carried them out. Atum spat forth Shu and vomited out Tefnut; but these, too, seem to be identified with Heart and Tongue, and were therefore also only aspects of Ptah's creative will. We have already seen that Tefnut was sometimes identified with the goddess Mayet, the spirit of world order. Thus Ptah was also seen as the establisher of a moral order and of royal power.

Horus, an aspect of Ptah – and personified in ritual as the reigning pharaoh, was declared in the Shabaka Stone to be ruler of the land and responsible for uniting it and naming it with the great name Tatenen. Now Tatenen was the name given in Memphis to Ptah ('Ptah of the primeval mound'), and the passage would therefore signify that Ptah not only created the land, but also that he *was* the land (just as in some versions Atum was declared actually to be the primeval mound, not simply to have been created on it). This, incidentally, was intended to confute the Heliopolitan claim that their temple stood on the primeval mound.

The Memphite theologians seem to have been aware that these personifications of Ptah were only symbols for quasi-philosophical ideas: that Ptah was the creative principle acting

through thought and will or command. In a variant of the Memphite system, Atum was relegated to still further insignificance: he was replaced as the agent of Ptah's will by Horus, who was the Heart, and by Thoth, who was the Tongue. This seems to be an attempt to incorporate even earlier beliefs than the Heliopolitan, for Horus was an ancient sun-god and Thoth the moon-god and the god of wisdom.

Ptah of Memphis was not only the universal and sole creator of the physical world, absorbing the functions of all the other gods; he also created an ethical order by creating the *ka* or soul of each being. In this respect the Memphite cosmogony seems to be more far-reaching than the Heliopolitan – but our knowledge of the latter may be incomplete. We are not told any more about Ptah's creative activity, but the Shabaka Stone text states that Ptah created everything, including the gods, and that he was also the origin of all good things – food and drink, offerings to the gods and every divine utterance (equivalent to divine acts of creation). It was recognised that his power was greater than that of all the other gods. He set the gods (who were, of course, aspects of his own divinity) in the places where their cults were practised; he established what offerings were to be made to them; he founded their shrines; and he created out of all the materials of his own being (i.e. the earth) the forms or images in which they were worshipped. The gods then entered into these forms and were content to rule together with their creator Ptah, Lord of the Two Lands. Ptah also established the cities and founded the nomes (provinces of Egypt), thus creating a political order.

Ptah was sometimes called the Divine Artificer as he was the supreme creator, and he was identified by the Greeks with their own god Hephaestus. But his function seems rather to have been as Lord of Truth: he was accompanied everywhere by Thoth, god of wisdom, and his works were the works of justice. 'Whereas he makes all things in a perfect manner, not deceptively, but artificially, together with Truth, he is called Ptah.'

The Memphite priests attempted also to associate their city with the Osiris cult, which was to gain prominence, by claiming that Memphis represented the site of the drowning and the burial of Osiris. As Osiris, like Ptah, was supposed to have taught mankind the arts of civilisation, it may be that the Memphite priests were attempting to assimilate Osiris within their own system.

The Hermopolitan Cosmogony

In Hermopolis, a city of Middle Egypt, a quite distinctive theory of creation was held which, it was claimed, was evolved earlier than any of the other cosmogonies. For the Heliopolitan Ennead, the Hermopolitans substituted an Ogdoad, or group of eight gods. These were Nun and his consort Naunet, Huh and his consort Hauhet, Kuk and his consort Kauket and Amon and his consort Amaunet. These eight gods together created the world. They then ruled over it for a period which was considered to be a golden age. After they had reigned for some time and they had completed their work of creation, the Eight died and went to the Underworld to live. Their power continued after their death, however, for they continued to cause the Nile to flow and the sun to rise each day.

Two of the Ogdoad, Nun and Amon, also figured in the other cosmogonies. The name of each of the goddesses was simply the feminine form of the name of the god whose consort she was; we may therefore treat these divinities as being only four in number. Etymologically, the names seem to have the following significance: Nun, water; Huh, unendingness; Kuk, darkness; and Amon, that which is unseen, or air. The four deities thus personify elements in creation legends concerning Nun which were told in the other cult centres. Nun was there described as an infinite watery waste, chaotic and dark. Amon, if he is to be regarded in the Hermopolitan legend as air or wind,

Bronze figure of Ptah. According to Memphite theology, Ptah was the creator of the universe. Though he later acquired funerary associations, his representation in mummy bandages is thought to have become fixed when sculptors were technically unable to produce separate limbs. He bears an *ankh* symbol in either hand and his sceptre is composed of the *djed* and the *uas*. Museo di Antichitá, Turin.

would then represent the force which stirred up the waters out of their stagnant immobility. The power of creation was thus immanent in Nun, but Amon was the essential force which set it in motion.

The four male deities of the Ogdoad were depicted in Egyptian art with frogs' heads, and the four female deities had serpents' heads. This would seem to derive from another tradition in Hermopolis which likened the eight primordial gods to the amphibious life which swarmed, apparently self-created, in the mud left behind by the annually receding Nile floodwaters. Thus instead of creating the primeval mound, the Eight would be conceived as hatching out on to it.

As in the other cult centres, the city was declared to be on the site of the primeval hill. In a park attached to the temple was a sacred lake called the 'Sea of the Two Knives' from which emerged the 'Isle of Flames'. This island was said to be the primeval hill and was a great place of pilgrimage and the setting for much ritual. Four variants of the creation myth as told at Hermopolis were connected with this lake and this island. In the first, the world was said to have originated in a cosmic egg (a concept not unlike that of the all-embracing Nun); this was laid by the celestial goose which first broke the silence of the world and was known as the 'Great Cackler'. The egg, laid on the primeval mound, contained the bird of light, Ra, who was to be creator of the world. Other sources said that the egg contained air – a tradition more in keeping with the Ogdoad legend. The remains of the egg were shown to pilgrims at Hermopolis.

The second version was similar to the first, except that in this case the egg was laid by an ibis – the bird representing Thoth, god of the moon and of wisdom. The cult of Thoth at Hermopolis was certainly established later than that of the Ogdoad, and it has therefore been suggested that this myth was an attempt by the Hermopolitan priests to graft the Thoth legend on to the older Ogdoad legend. Thoth himself was said to be

self-created, the Ogdoad being his souls.

The third variant of the Hermopolitan doctrine reverted to the imagery of creation out of the waters, and was exceptionally poetic. According to this version, a lotus flower rose out of the waters of the 'Sea of the Two Knives'. When its petals opened the calyx of the flower was seen to bear a divine child, who was Ra.

The fourth version of this legend was that the lotus opened to reveal a scarab beetle (symbol of the sun); the scarab then transformed itself into a boy, who wept; and finally his tears became mankind. This was another way of saying that men were the children of Ra. Indeed in Hermopolis the lotus was sometimes specifically identified with the Eye of Ra. The lotus is a flower which opens and closes every day: it could therefore easily be associated with the cult of the sun-god, which it bore within its petals. By opening his Eye, Ra was said to separate day from night. While men emerged from Ra's eyes, the lesser gods came forth from his mouth.

The Ogdoad were said to be responsible for the flow of the Nile and the daily rise of the sun; they were also said to have created the lotus bearing the sun-god, and this lotus rose out of the waters – always a source of fecundity in Egypt and in this case no doubt associated with the waters of Nun. It may be seen, therefore, that these myths are easily reconciled with each other and constitute poetic variants rather than conflicting stories. Not even Hermopolitan legend, however, was without anomalies. Thus the text states that 'out of the lotus, created by the Eight, came forth Ra, who created *all things*, divine and human'.

The Theban Cosmogony

The chief god of Thebes, a city of Upper Egypt which was the seat of the centralised government in the New Kingdom (1570-1085 B.C.), was called Amon, and had absorbed the indigenous god Mont. The gods of the other chief cult centres had already become established as high gods throughout Egypt and had considerable popularity among the people, who by this time had come to share in the benefits of the formerly exclusive religion. It was therefore essential for the priests of Thebes, if they were to command support for the advance of their deity to the position of chief god, that they should incorporate the main features of the important earlier cosmogonies.

Amon, who also figured in the Hermopolitan myths, was associated with the air as an invisible, dynamic force; it was thus easy to identify him with the power of the supreme and invisible creator. Theban doctrine incorporated in Amon aspects of all the other creator-gods. It stated that Thebes was the first city, after which all the others were later modelled. Thebes was the site of the first water, Nun, and of the first land, the primeval mound. The city was founded on the hill and in this way the world began. Then mankind was created in order to found other cities after the pattern of Thebes. Thebes was the Eye of Ra, and it oversaw all the other cities (just as the Eye of Atum oversaw Shu and Tefnut in the waters of Nun).

Like Atum, Amon created himself: there was no other god to create him, and he had neither father nor mother. He was invisible, born in secret. All the other gods came into being after he had performed the first creative act. Just as Ptah was said to embody other gods as facets of his own divine nature, so the Theban Amon embraced whole cosmogonies as aspects or phases of his creative activity. Thus the first of his forms was said to be the Ogdoad of Hermopolis; his next form was as Tatenen, the primeval mound of Memphis, in which form he created the first gods. Amon then left the earth to abide in heaven as Ra (a Hermopolitan belief). He also took the form of the divine child revealed by the opening petals of the lotus in the midst of Nun. Like Ra or Horus, his eyes lit the earth. Like Thoth, he was the moon. He made men and created the gods, organising the Ennead and setting up the members of the Ogdoad as his divine fathers and priests, with Shu at their head and

Opposite. A limestone tablet dedicated to Thoth, god of letters and scribe of the gods, chronographer and great magician, whom Hermopolitan myth sometimes called the demiurge. Usually represented as an ibis, Thoth was also god of the moon and is seen here with a winged moon over his head. British Museum, London.

Above. The four deities of the sanctuary of the Great Temple at Abu Simbel: Ptah, Amon, Rameses II and Ra-Harakhte. The plinth in the foreground supported the sacred barque in which Amon was borne forth among the people. Rameses dedicated his Great Temple principally to Amon, while nearby the lesser temple of his queen, Nefertari, was dedicated to Hathor.

Tefnut as the concubine of god. As in Hermopolitan belief, Amon was the vital force which roused Nun from his torpor and started the creative cycle.

The priests of Thebes also claimed that their city was the birthplace of Osiris, no doubt because by this time Osiris had attained such popularity and was associated with the well-being of the royal house and the fertility of the land.

Other Cosmogonic Notions

Like many primitive peoples, the ancient Egyptians seem early on to have worshipped a universal mother-goddess. She took many forms, and her tradition can be traced in a number of goddesses who survived into the pantheon of historical times. The background of a mother-goddess tradition often explains the particular form taken by myths in which these goddesses were involved. It may well be that this deity was supposed to have been the creator of the entire world. Thus Nut, or Hathor, was said to have been the mother of Ra; Geb was her bull and Ra their son; men, in turn, were sometimes called the 'cattle of Ra'. Alternatively, Hathor's son was the 'bull of confusion' Ihy who, having only one parent, was similar to Shu. Ihy was a symbol of

a fresh beginning. Again Isis, though originally only the consort of Osiris, was made the mother of Horus, from whom was descended every pharaoh – and on whom in turn the lives of all his subjects depended. Neith, the goddess of Sais in the Delta, was no doubt also such a deity, though she was primarily a warlike goddess. She was referred to as the oldest of the deities, and as such the gods appealed to her for judgement during the Great Quarrel between Set and Horus.

Khnum, a god perhaps later absorbed by Amon, but who survived as an independent deity in Elephantine, near the First Cataract of the Nile, was said to have created men from clay and straw and to have fashioned them on a potter's wheel. As early as the Old Kingdom, in the *Pyramid Texts*, the pharaoh was described as the son of Khnum; and the notion occurs again in a much later text, of the seventh to sixth century B.C., which declares that 'man is clay and straw'. This could mean that mankind, together with the entire animal world, had emerged from the sun-dried mud of the Nile, thus bypassing the agency of the gods of the Ennead. However, it should be noted that in a bas-relief from the temple at Luxor dedicated to Amon-Ra by the Eighteenth-Dynasty Amenhotep III, Khnum may be shown fashioning the infant pharaoh and his *ka* on his potter's wheel, but this follows intercourse between the god Amon and Queen Mutemuia, and it is left to the goddess Hathor to animate the potter's manikins by touching them with the *ankh*, symbol of life.

At a very late, Roman, stage Khnum was once more elevated in rank. On temple inscriptions dating from the first and second centuries A.D. at Esna in Upper Egypt, he is identified with Ra and described as fashioner of men and cattle and of the beneficent god (the pharaoh, no doubt), who orders the land and ensures that seeds shall grow fruitfully.

The Deities

The cosmic gods, as we have seen, were adopted with particular interest by the theologians of the great cult centres and were woven into the cosmogonies that supported the official state religion. Except in so far as these gods absorbed the characteristics of local gods, they tended to receive little popular worship: the gods of the pharaoh were traditionally unapproachable by the masses. But this was changed by religious democratisation in later periods, and the rise to prominence of the ancient Osirian deities. The god Bes, for example, originally cast as protective deity of the pharaoh, became one of the most popular cult figures. At all periods we know most about the gods of the kingdom: those worshipped by the pharaohs and those which attained nationwide prominence. Though in the reign of Thuthmosis III the number of gods worshipped was said to be seven hundred and forty, most of these were city gods of whom we know little. In the following study we shall touch on them only where they became absorbed by the great gods and entered the common mythology.

Divinities of the 'First Time'

Nun

Nun (or Nu) was chaos, or the primordial waste of waters in which all creation was immanent, and was guarded by four bisexual frog and serpent-headed deities. Atum rose from Nun, who was therefore called 'father of the gods', though his son was greater than he was himself. In Hermopolis Nun was called 'Infinity, Nothingness, Nowhere and Darkness'. He was represented as a bearded man or sometimes with the head of a frog, a beetle or a serpent, standing up to his waist in water and holding up his arms to support the solar barque, in which the sun-disk was being raised up by a scarab. The scarab was supported by Isis and Nephthys and the crew of the boat included Shu and Geb; these were described in the accompanying texts as the gods who issued from Nun. But in the texts Nun is said to have no surface, for in the primordial scheme he filled the whole cosmos; it was only the intervention of Shu, the air, which separated the sky from the surface of the earth.

Nun was regarded as still existing, for he was the water found when digging deep, as for a well, and he was the turbulent floodwaters of the Nile. It was sometimes believed that the waters of Nun, which surrounded the floating earth, would one day re-envelop the world and that Atum would revert to his original form as a serpent; Osiris, instead of Ra, would then sail over the waters of Nun. In general, however, Nun was a beneficent god, for he looked after Shu and Tefnut at birth and he was supposed to guard and keep in check the demonic powers of chaos represented by serpents.

Atum

Atum (or Tem or Tum) was an early god of Heliopolis and a predynastic sun-deity. The Heliopolitan theologians interpreted his name to mean 'complete one', a reference to their belief that he created himself out of the waters of Nun by an effort of will or by the power of the spoken word – by uttering his own name. They also

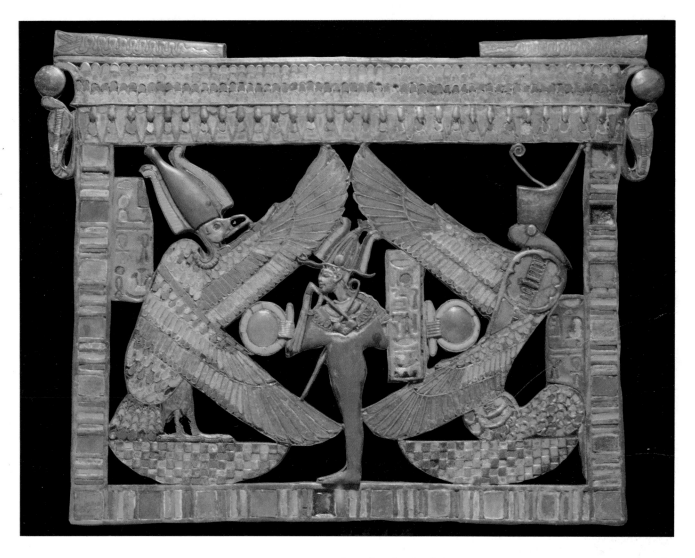

The deities of the kingdom. On the left is the vulture-goddess Nekhebet wearing the white crown of Upper Egypt. On the right is the cobra-goddess Edjo of the Delta, wearing the red crown of Lower Egypt. They flank Osiris, who forsook rule on earth to become Lord of the Afterlife, and with whom dead pharaohs were identified. Pectoral of Tutankhamon. Eighteenth Dynasty. Egyptian Museum, Cairo.

called him Neb-er-djer, 'Lord to the Limit' or Universal God.

As we have seen, he was the founder of the Heliopolitan Ennead, and was called Bull of the Ennead – a reference to his cult animal the bull Mnevis. Atum was sometimes thought to have originated as a ser-pent in Nun and to be destined to return to that form; but through his identification with Ra, serpents be-came his enemies. He was sometimes represented with the head of an ich-neumon because once, when a serpent attacked him, he turned himself into an ichneumon in order to devour it.

More commonly, however, he was represented as a bearded man, usually aged and tottering to the western hor-izon as the setting sun. As creator of the gods and men and hence of the divine order in heaven and on earth, he was called Lord of the Two Lands and as such was depicted wearing the *pschent*, the double crown of Upper and Lower Egypt, and bearing the *ankh* sceptre, the sign of life and sym-bol of royal authority.

Originally bisexual, and as Iusau sole parent of the first divine couple, Shu and Tefnut, Atum was later given two wives – Iusas and Nebhet Hotep.

Ra

Ra (or Re or Phra) was the god per-sonifying the sun in its strength, his name meaning simply sun. He was early identified with Atum the creator-god of Heliopolis, his chief cult centre. Thus though sometimes Atum was considered to have created Ra, more often Ra was said to have emerged from Nun by the effort of his own will. It was thought that he rose from the primeval waters en-closed within the petals of a lotus blossom, which enfolded him once more when he returned to it each night; or that he rose in the shape of a phoenix, the Bennu bird, and alighted on the pyramidal top of an obelisk, the Benben stone, which sym-bolised a ray of the sun. The most sacred object of the temple of Ra at Heliopolis was this Benben stone, whose gilded surfaces caught and re-flected the morning sun. The site of

the temple was said to be the primordial hill itself, and the House of the Benben was at its centre.

Sometimes Ra was said to have a consort, Rat, or Iusas, or Urt-Hikeu ('Great in Magic'), or even Hathor; but more often, like Atum, he was said to have produced on his own the first divine couple, Shu and Tefnut. They in turn produced Geb and Nut, whose children were Osiris and Isis, Set and Nephthys. Alternatively Ra himself was said to be the son of Geb and Nut in the form of a cow. Each morning Ra was born as a calf, grew to be a bull by midday, when he fertilised his mother as Kamephis ('Bull of his mother'), and died in the evening, to be reborn as his own son next morning. Further beliefs were that he was hatched from an egg formed of clay by Ptah or laid by Geb in the

form of a goose. Hathor was sometimes said to be Ra's child, as were Osiris, Set, Horus and Mayet.

Ra was called 'father of the gods' and their head or king. He was also said to be father of mankind, and of all other living creatures, which were thought to have grown from his sweat and tears. The tears were shed by Ra's Eye, whose peculiarity was that it was separable from him and had a mind of its own. One day it failed to return so Ra sent Shu and Tefnut to fetch it back; the Eye resisted and in the struggle shed tears. From these tears grew men – perhaps a play on words, since 'tears' and 'men' had a similar sound in Egyptian.

A variant of this myth has already been recounted, that the Eye was sent by Atum to seek out Shu and Tefnut when they were lost in the dark

waters of Nun. On that occasion the Eye was rewarded by being placed on Atum's forehead. Yet another variant has it that the Eye wandered away of its own accord and Ra sent Thoth, the moon, to fetch it back; when the Eye, or sun, returned to Ra it found to its fury that it had been replaced by another Eye (perhaps also the moon). Thoth, however, mollified the original Eye, and Ra pacified it by placing it, in the shape of the *uraeus* serpent, on his brow 'where it could rule the whole world'. The Eye, or *uraeus*, was to become the effective ruler of the world, and as such was to be worn by the pharaohs as a symbol of their majesty and their descent from the sun god.

At the beginning, however, Ra himself ruled on earth over the universe he had created. His reign was a sort of golden age, known to the Egyptians as the 'First Time', when men and gods lived together on earth. When Ra was young and vigorous he maintained firm rule, and the power of divine order, Mayet, was uncontested. Ra's daily routine was immutable. After his toilet and the breakfast brought by the morning star, re-enacted later in the temple ritual, Ra would set out from the House of the Benben in Heliopolis and, accompanied by Shu, would progress majestically through the twelve provinces (daylight hours) of his realm. Sometimes his close inspection became oppressive to his people and they rebelled, as against the summer heat; but they were powerless against the mighty king. On one occasion the serpent Apep conspired with Ra's enemies to kill him at sunrise, but they were overcome in a battle lasting all day. On another Ra took the form of a cat or lion to behead Apep.

As Ra grew old, however, his power waned; he became an old man, incontinent, and dribbled from his trembling mouth. Occasionally one of the deities sought to take advantage of his senility. As we shall relate, Isis was the most nearly successful, and Osiris too was sometimes in conflict with him. We shall see in the legend

of the great quarrel between Horus and Set (which may well relate to the prehistoric rivalries that ended with unification under Horus-worshiping pharaohs) that all the other gods were impatient with Ra as judge.

Eventually men too became aware of Ra's weakness and plotted against him, saying: 'His Majesty is grown old. His bones are silver, his flesh is gold and his hair real lapis lazuli.' But Ra knew what was going on and secretly summoned the gods, his ministers of state, to advise him on how to put down the rebellion. One by one the gods gave their opinions and Nun spoke for them all in saying that his son Ra was still great, greater than his father, and still commanded fear. He should remain on his throne and turn his Eye on the rebels. Men thereupon took refuge in the mountains; but Ra sent out his Eye in the shape of his daughter Hathor or Sekhmet, a lioness. Hathor soon subdued mankind and was eager to destroy it altogether. But Ra was just, wishing to uphold the divine order of his creation and the balance between gods and men, so he restrained Hathor.

Nevertheless Ra now felt pain and weariness after all these troubles and wished to withdraw from the world. He therefore mounted on Nut as a

cow and she raised him into the heavens. The other gods clung to her belly and became the stars. In this way heaven and earth, gods and men were separated and the present world was created. The sun god Ra abdicated his position as ruler of the world in favour of the moon-god Thoth, who brought light back to mankind. This was how the Egyptians explained the daily disappearance of the sun in the evening and its replacement by the moon. In his bounty Ra provided mankind, through Thoth, with protective spells to keep them from harm on earth, and his heavenly kingdom became an afterworld where they could hope for eternal bliss. Other myths declared that Thoth was the scribe only and that the throne of earth was passed to Geb, or to Shu and Geb, and that of the heavens to Nut. These new rulers governed with the help of the Ennead.

From the time when Ra returned to the heavens, an immutable order was

Above. Ra in the form of a cat beheading the serpent Apep and so defeating the foes of Neb-er-djer (Atum) and ensuring the triumph of light over darkness. Behind him is the sacred persea tree, the point from which the sun rises each morning. *Book of the Dead*, Papyrus of the scribe Ani. Nineteenth Dynasty, c. 1250 B.C. British Museum, London.

Opposite. Ibis-headed statuette of Thoth, who as god of justice ably defended Osiris (whose emblems he wears here) before the tribunal of the gods, during the eighty-year wrangle for the throne between Horus and Set. As inventor of speech as well as writing, Thoth refuted the claims of Set, which were basically that might was right. British Museum, London.

established for him. The world was bounded by mountains which supported the sky and at whose foot was Naunet, the consort of Nun in Hermopolitan doctrine. It was from these mountains that Ra appeared. The sun was therefore reborn daily either from the watery abyss or alternatively as son of the sky-goddess. He emerged in the east from behind Manu, the mountain of sunrise, and passing between two sycamores, began his journey across the sky in what was called the Manjet-boat, or 'Barque of Millions of Years'. Ra was accompanied by a number of gods who acted as the boat's crew. These included Geb and Thoth and the personifications of various aspects of the sun's power, especially Hu – authoritative utterance, i.e. command and creation by divine (or royal) decree; Sia – intelligence; and Hike – magic. Horus too was sometimes a member of the crew, standing at the helm of the boat while Thoth stood at its prow destroying all Ra's enemies. As he sailed across the sky, Ra wore the double crown of Egypt, which combined the red crown of Lower Egypt and the white crown of Upper Egypt. As on the crown of the pharaohs, the *uraeus* serpent was seen at the front rearing its head and spitting fire at all enemies.

The chief of Ra's enemies was Apep, or Apophis, a huge serpent which lived in the waters of Nun or in the depths of the celestial Nile and who each day attempted to obstruct the passage of the solar barque. This was a serious challenge to Ra, and it has been suggested that in this legend Apep represented the earlier and discarded form of the sun-god himself, when he was lying in the waters of Nun before he began the creation of the world. This would explain Apep's strength and his particular resentment of the daily journey of the sun across the sky; it would also explain why in these daily battles Ra was always ultimately victorious. In the myth of the great quarrel, Set claimed that it was he who stood in the prow of the solar barque and vanquished all the enemies of Ra and cast them back into the abyss. Stormy weather would be interpreted by the Egyptians as a momentary victory of the serpent Apep. Likewise when there was a total eclipse the Egyptians imagined that Apep had swallowed the solar barque.

It was sometimes thought that Ra was born in the morning as a child, grew to maturity by midday, and by evening had become a doddering old man who would die that night. This legend corresponded to the myth of his reign on earth. Accordingly, when Ra embarked on his night voyage he was given the name Auf-Ra or Auf, which meant 'flesh' or 'corpse'. For his journey through the twelve hours of darkness Ra sailed in another boat, the Mesektet-boat or night-barque. This boat was sometimes represented as a serpent with a head at either end. As during the day, Ra was accompanied by a crew of gods, which again included Hu, Sia and Hike. During the night, the god Upuaut, Opener of the Ways, stood at the prow of the barque.

According to another belief, the souls of dead pharaohs (and later of other men) in the form of stars served as the crew of the solar barques. 'Those who can never set' were the stars which do not set during the day

but are invisible because of the sun's brilliance; they formed the day crew. 'Those who can never become weary' were the stars which are visible for only a short time during the night; these were the night crew and they were imagined to slip away one by one towards the West (the Underworld to the Egyptians), where they joined the night-barque in its journey through the invisible part of the world, which was called the Duat.

During the twelve hours of the night the perils which Ra faced were even greater than those he faced during the day. Again he was confronted by his eternal enemy, the serpent Apep. But in the underworld each of the twelve provinces which Ra had to visit during the hours of darkness was peopled by monstrous serpents and demons who threatened the existence of the dead as personified in the dead sun-god Auf. Like the souls of the dead human beings, the previous forms of the sun-god, Atum, Ra and Khepri, were said to be buried in the Underworld. As Auf passed along the infernal river, the various gods and demons which inhabited each province of the Underworld came forward to tow his barque, for no wind could penetrate into the Duat. They were under the direction of the goddess of

the hour, who opened the gate leading into the next hour with a password known to her alone. But these were not friendly spirits. They were monstrous creatures which took the forms of serpents with two heads at either end, as in the fourth province, or of a huge serpent whose back bore the heads of four bearded men. This last serpent, which inhabited the sixth province, was called the 'devourer of spirits' and was said to be invisible to Auf. The four men on his back were the sons of Horus – Imset, Hapy, Duamutef and Qebehsenuf – which were the deities presiding over the Canopic jars in which after embalmment the lungs, liver, stomach and intestines of a dead man were preserved. The serpent himself was said to devour the defeated enemies of Ra and Osiris. In later Osirian belief, this creature took a different form, Ammut, and devoured the souls of those not 'true of voice'.

This brief description of some of the inhabitants of the twelve provinces will give an idea of the mysterious terror and invisible perils represented by the realm of the Underworld in the solar myths; as we shall see when we consider the Osiris cult, the Underworld was later to become a realm where a man might

Above. The sun's disk, enclosed by the *uraeus*, resting on the shoulders of two animals with the feather of truth on their heads. On the right is a mythical creature of the Underworld. British Museum, London.

Opposite top. A papyrus painting showing the sun being rolled along its course by an enormous scarab. On the left is Auf-Ra in the Mesektet-boat, with Geb in the prow and Khepri ready to take his place at dawn, being drawn along the solar course through the underworld by the gods of the hours of the night. British Museum, London.

Opposite below. Ra, the sun-god, in the Barque of Millions of Years in which he traversed the heavens. He wears on his head, and accompanies, a vast sun-disk symbolising his powers as lord of the heavens. The boat, formed of a serpent, bears his Eye; and the god is seated on a pedestal representing Mayet, the divine order. From the Theban *Book of the Dead,* Papyrus of Ani, Nineteenth Dynasty. British Museum, London.

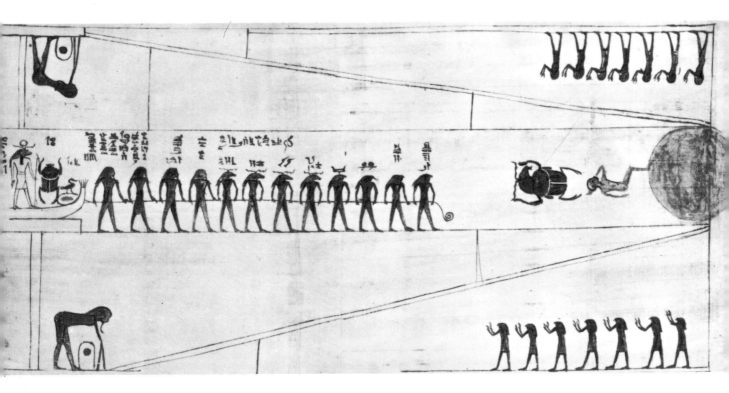

hope for eternal life. But even when these beliefs prevailed, spells and magic incantations had to be said by the living to preserve the dead soul from the threatening demons by which it was attacked on its passage. Part of the role of Auf in the Underworld was briefly to shed light on the souls of the dead as he passed through their realm. He would pass from cavern to cavern, receiving the acclamations of the inhabitants of the Underworld, who waited with impatience for the light he bore, and after his departure fell back once

more into the agony of darkness.

Having overcome all the perils of the Underworld, including the serpent Apep, who was pierced with knives and bound in chains, the sun-god reached the twelfth province. This was sometimes thought to have the form of a serpent, through whose body Auf-Ra passed in order to be born from its mouth, as he was born daily from Nut. So he rose once more to shine upon the earth. The gods of his retinue dragged up his barque (the Manjet-boat), and the sun-god was reunited with Khepri and rose once

more into the sky. The form of Auf was discarded and was seen lying to the side. Shu, the god of air, was seen ready to take the sun's disk into his outstretched arms, just as at evening the solar disk was handed from one boat to another by the goddess of the east to the goddess of the west.

Such were the most widely held ideas about the daily solar cycle; but other notions persisted, perhaps chiefly among the common people. One was that Ra was the son of the sky-goddess Nut, who was represented as a cow. Ra was imagined as

Above. Mummy lying on its bier and receiving life and warmth from the rays of the sun. In the early solar mythology Auf-Ra briefly shed light on the inhabitants of the Underworld each night as he passed through its caverns. Painting from the coffin of Besenmut, a priest of Mont at Thebes. Twenty-sixth Dynasty. British Museum, London.

Opposite. Painting from the Papyrus of Ani showing Ra and the Herd of Heaven. At the close of each day the Solar god of Heliopolis began his voyage through the regions of darkness. The herd, seven cows and a bull, provided sustenance on the journey. Early Nineteenth Dynasty. British Museum, London.

a calf born anew every morning and swallowed up by his mother, the sky-goddess, every evening. This would explain why when Ra-Atum decided to withdraw from the world after the near-destruction of mankind, he was borne up to the heavens by the cow-goddess Nut. The sun was also imagined sometimes to be the son of Nun: in Hermopolitan doctrine he was said to rise each morning from the opening petals of a lotus flower floating on the waters of Nun, and as the petals of the lotus closed

again in the evening Ra would be enfolded within them.

Ra was sometimes represented as a simple disk borne on a boat, but he was most frequently depicted as a falcon-headed man because of his identification with Horus, a former high god of Egypt who either was the sun or whose right eye was the sun. The head was crowned with a sun-disk encircled by the *uraeus* spitting fire at Ra's enemies, and the god, in this guise known as Ra-Harakhte, bore the *ankh* and *uas* sceptres. Auf

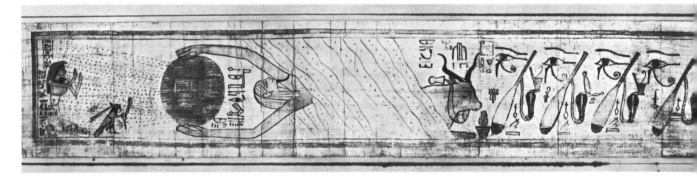

was similarly depicted, except that the sun-disk was borne between the horns of a ram – possibly borrowed from Khnum or from the sacred ram of Mendes, which was considered to be the soul of Osiris. Ra was also represented as the divine child in the lotus flower; as the Bennu bird, which rose at dawn from the Benben stone and with its voice heralded the good tidings of creation; as a falcon; as a lion or cat – the form in which he dismembered Apep; as the bull Kamephis, or the bull Mnevis; or simply as an old man, seated or walking, whose head was surmounted by the solar disk, around which was wreathed the *uraeus*. In this last form he was usually considered as Atum, the setting sun.

Ra was closely identified with the pharaohs, of whom he was the protective deity. The pharaoh was thought to be Horus son of Ra and to become Ra after his death. At first the pharaoh alone was allowed to worship Ra; but the god became less awesome when others were allowed to contemplate him, and at the same time became the state god rather than just the pharaoh's god. The pharaoh now became Horus son of Osiris rather than Horus the sun.

Some of the myths showed Ra as weak or even ridiculous – god of the gods and yet the victim of circumstances who intervened only when absolutely necessary. Nevertheless he maintained his power as chief state god in one or other of his many manifestations or assimilations with other gods, even at the height of Osirianism, because of his close identification with the royal house as upholder of moral and political order in this life. Ra was revered at the temples of all the other gods because the chief priest at each of these shrines was the divine pharaoh, and the cults there were modelled on that of Ra at Heliopolis. One of the principal features of the cult was the ritual cleansing, symbolic of Ra's purity as creator, as upholder of truth on earth and as judge of the dead.

According to the Heliopolitans, the wife of a priest of Ra was selected by Ra as his wife. After his union with her in the form of her husband she bore three sons who were to become the first three pharaohs of the Fifth Dynasty. Thereafter all pharaohs were considered to be actual sons of Ra. Thus the pharaohs were able to claim not only that they had been handed down their authority in direct succession from Horus (i.e. Horus the sun, not Horus son of Osiris), but that they were so closely linked with the sun that their line partook of the sun's inevitable rebirth after death. Royal commands were thus of divine authority. As he was sole mediator between Ra and the people of Egypt, the pharaoh could expect that the people would take very seriously their duty to ensure by prayers that his soul passed safely through the perils of the Underworld. For just as it was essential for the fertility and well-being of the land of Egypt and its peoples that the sun should rise every morning, so it was essential that the soul of the dead pharaoh should be protected and that his son, the new incarnation of Ra, should be equally respected. When later the dead pharaoh was identified with Osiris, it was said that Ra sent Anubis down to piece together the dismembered Osiris, thus permitting his resurrection. Osiris and Ra then ruled conjointly in heaven and in the Underworld.

Khepri

Khepri (or Khepera) was an aspect of Ra, personifying the young sun at dawn welcoming Auf at the end of the night journey. He was the rising sun, whose name meant both 'He who comes into existence' and 'Scarab'. The scarab beetle can be seen pushing along in front of it a ball of food which it buries in order to be able to eat it unmolested. The Egyptians thought that this ball was the egg which the female scarab lays in a ball of her own dung. They therefore took the scarab as a symbol for the self-generative aspect of the sun-god, for they conceived of the scarab as being born out of its own substance. Because of his power of self-renewal Khepri was sometimes identified with the creator, Neb-er-djer or Atum, and was associated with the Osirian afterlife. He was represented as a scarab-headed man or as a scarab pushing the disk of the new sun before him. Sometimes yesterday's sun was depicted behind him.

Shu

Shu and his twin sister Tefnut formed the first divine couple of the Heliopolitan Ennead, and were created by Ra. Shu was the personification of the

atmosphere and his name, meaning 'to raise', derived from his most important act in mythology, the separation of his children, Geb, the earth, and Nut, the sky, which resulted in the creation of the world as men knew it. On the orders of Ra or, according to some, spurred by incestuous jealousy, Shu thrust himself between Geb and Nut, thus breaking their close embrace. Alternatively Shu was said to have been ordered by Ra to support Nut when, as a cow, she had become dizzy after raising Ra to the heights of heaven.

Shu was usually represented as a bearded man standing or kneeling over Geb with arms upraised to support Nut. On his head he wore an ostrich feather, the hieroglyph of his name, or four tall plumes, symbolising the four pillars of heaven which supported Nut. Sometimes he was represented as a lion, or as a column of air.

Shu's name is also said to mean 'to be empty' and he was treated in some texts as emptiness deified. In others he was accorded rather more importance: as god of air, Shu was seen in the later texts as personifying the divine intelligence. He therefore became the immediate agent of Atum's creation, and hence an embodiment of Atum's supreme power. Shu was thus the god who set creation in motion, forming the world by separating earth and sky. From this legend arose some dispute as to whether Nun, Atum or Shu was the oldest of the gods, and some Egyptian theologians seem to have thought that all three were born simultaneously. Shu was sometimes thought of as god of light and shown bearing the solar disk – rather than Nut – aloft. In some New Kingdom texts he was equated with Ra-Harakhte.

Though Thoth was sometimes said to have succeeded Ra as king on earth, Shu was more generally thought to be his father's successor. He built many temples to the gods throughout the land, all of which faced the four pillars of heaven, his palace on the eastern horizon. This palace, called Het Nebes, was a mighty and impenetrable shrine; but

the sons of Apep, who dwelt in the desert, attacked Egypt and wrought great destruction, though they were unable to storm the shrines and were defeated and driven back by the gods.

After this, however, Shu fell ill and lost his sight. Dissension broke out in his palace and misfortunes befell the kingdom. At the same time, Shu's son Geb fell in love with his own mother Tefnut and took to wandering about, disconsolate. Finally he returned to the palace during the daytime while his father was in heaven, violated Tefnut and seized the throne. Shu dared not return and darkness and storms filled the land.

Tefnut

Tefnut, Shu's sister and wife and said to share one soul with him, was the personification of life-giving dew and moisture. Her tears, which fell to the ground as she helped her husband support the sky, were turned into incense-bearing plants. In the Memphite cosmogony, Tefnut was identified with the Tongue of Ptah, or symbol of the means to creation; in this function she partnered her brother Shu as an embodiment of the supreme divine power. Alternatively, she was sometimes identified with the goddess Mayet, the spirit of world order, whereby she acquired an even more positive spiritual significance.

Tefnut also had a solar character and with Shu each morning received the newborn sun as it broke free from the eastern mountains. She was sometimes considered to be the left eye of Horus, and as Eye of Ra once escaped into the desert of Nubia in the shape of a lioness or lynx. Ra sent Shu, in the form of a lion, and Thoth to fetch her back. Having changed themselves into baboons, they tracked her down near the Mountain of Sunrise, the birthplace of Osiris, and Thoth overcame her with magic. Her marriage to Shu was said to have taken place after this, but sometimes she was held to have married Thoth on their return from Nubia, when Ra placed Tefnut on his brow as the fierce *uraeus* serpent.

Tefnut was therefore depicted as a lioness or with the head of a lion

wearing the solar disk and the *uraeus*. Occasionally, when she was considered as protectress of Ra and the pharaoh, she was shown as the *uraeus* itself. She was also protectress of Osiris and of the dead identified with him.

Anhur

Anhur (or Onuris) was identified with Shu after he had brought back Tefnut from Nubia, and his name meant 'He who brought back the far-off', or 'Support of the heavens'. A variant of the myth had it that the Eye of Horus in the form of the lioness-goddess Sekhmet was stolen by a gazelle and taken off to the Nubian desert. Anhur, god of Thinis and Sebennytos, near Abydos, recovered the Eye. On his return he married the lioness, who was then called Mehit or Mai-hesa.

Anhur was therefore closely identified with Horus the Warrior and was depicted as a prince clothed in a long tunic and with one or both hands raised, or smiting his enemies from a war chariot. Like Shu, he wore four tall plumes on his head. He was regarded as a protector against enemies, evil spirits and harmful animals.

His cult became widespread and extremely popular from the New Kingdom right through to Ptolemaic times, unlike that of Shu, and ordinary people referred to him as the deliverer who would defend them and bear their human burdens – thus domesticating the aspect of his solar associations and the connections with Osirianism arising from his proximity to Abydos.

Geb

Geb (or Keb), the earth, was generally thought to be the son of Shu and Tefnut and with his twin sister Nut to have formed the second divine couple. Sometimes, however, he was said to be the father of Ra the sun and Thoth the moon and was called 'father of the gods'. Before the creation of the present universe, Geb lay with Nut in a close embrace. But Ra was displeased at this and ordered Shu to separate them. With their separation space and light were created.

Geb was the earth itself, and his body as he was pictured lying below Nut, propped up on an elbow and with knee bent, constituted the mountains and valleys of the earth's surface. The green patches or plants seen on his body in papyri symbolised his aspect as vegetation-god. Geb was also sometimes represented as a goose, 'the Great Cackler', or with a goose on his head, for in this form he was said to have laid the egg from which hatched the sun as Bennu bird. At other times he was seen as the 'bull of Nut'. Geb and Nut were the parents of Osiris and Isis, Set and Nephthys.

Sometimes it was said that Ra or Atum handed the throne of earth directly to Geb, appointing Nut as queen of heaven. But more generally Geb was thought to have been the third divine king, having ousted his father Shu.

The storms and darkness which followed Geb's seizure of the throne and violation of his mother persisted for nine days; but then they cleared and Geb was acknowledged as king. He suffered, however, for his unlawful usurpation. After seventy-five days he set out to visit the various parts of his kingdom and in the east was told of the great valour of his father and of how Shu had fortified himself by placing the *uraeus* serpent on his head. Geb resolved to put the serpent on his own head and reached out to open the chest in which it was kept. But the serpent immediately breathed forth deadly venom; all Geb's attendants were killed by it and Geb was burned and afflicted with fever. No medicines could cure him, so the gods advised him to contemplate the *aart* of Ra. The *aart* was set in a stone coffer on Geb's head and the fever

abated. Some years later, when the *aart* was washed in the sacred lake near Het Nebes, it was transformed into a crocodile, Sebek, and slipped away into the water.

Geb now wished to reign according to the divine tradition established by his predecessors and asked his councillors about the temple-building, the establishment of nomes and settlements, the town and wall construction and the irrigation works of his father. Having learnt all the details, Geb declared that he would make good the ravages of the last years of his father's reign, just as Shu had striven on behalf of his father Atum. This he did, building many more temples and establishing order and prosperity.

When he had lived for 1,773 years, Geb decided to abdicate in favour of Horus and Set, assigning the North to Horus and the South to Set. As we shall see, Set's objections – for he wished to inherit the whole kingdom – gave rise to a prolonged feud.

Geb assumed Thoth's place as herald and judge in Ra's kingdom. It was sometimes said to be Geb, not Ra, who as presiding judge at the trial to settle the dispute between Horus and Set assigned the throne to Horus. This was the first trial after Geb's ascent to heaven. Geb acted also as a member of Ra's crew in the solar barque. In memory of Geb's great reign on earth, the royal throne was known as the 'throne of Geb'.

Nut

Nut, goddess of the sky, was often represented as a woman with an elongated body arched over the earth. She was supported by Shu, so that only her fingertips and toes touched the earth. Though separated from Geb during the day, she descended to him each night, thus creating darkness. When storms occurred during the day, Nut was thought to have slipped part of the way down the four pillars or the circle of mountains that supported her.

As we have remarked, Geb was sometimes said to be the father of the sun and the moon; Nut too was associated with them – either as their mother or as a great cow whose eyes

they formed. Ra· seems to have been jealous, whether as grandfather or as son, and forbade Nut to marry Geb. When she did so, he ordained that she should be unable to bear children in any given month of the year. But Thoth was sorry for her and by playing draughts with the moon won from him a seventy-second part of his light. This amounted to five days, the five intercalated days before the New Year in the Egyptian calendar. On each of these days consecutively Nut was able to give birth to a child: Osiris, Horus, Set, Isis and Nephthys.

In fact Nut was said to have numerous children, for she was originally a mother-goddess. The hieroglyph for her name, which she wore on her head when depicted as a woman, is thought to be a womb as well as a waterpot. She was sometimes pictured as a sow whose belly was covered with countless sucking-pigs, the stars, which she swallowed every morning. The other common representation was as a beautiful cow, the form she took when Ra-Atum had wearied of his rebellious kingdom on earth and Nun requested her to bear him up into the heavens. As she rose higher and higher, Nut began to tremble, so a god was appointed to steady each of her four legs, those chosen being Horus, Set, Thoth and Sopdu, representing the four quarters of the earth. Shu supported Nut's belly, which became the heavenly ocean or river along which sailed the solar barque.

She was in fact the mother as well as the daughter of Ra, for in various fashions the sun was said to be reborn each morning from her womb. This was symbolised by her presence at the emergence of Khepri from the Underworld, when she would reach down to take the scarab from the solar barque held up from the abyssal waters by Nun. The blood she shed in giving birth to the sun was said to colour the sky pink at dawn.

Through association with Khepri, the reborn, resurrected sun, Nut became identified as protectress of the dead, who were pictured lying in her starry bosom. In this role she had wings which she spread over them.

The firmament of her body was painted on the inner lid of coffins so that the soul of the deceased might join the blessed dead.

Osiris

Osiris was an ancient corn-deity whose followers, coming probably from Syria, identified their god with a pastoral deity called Andjeti and set

49

themselves up in his city in the Delta in predynastic times. Their cult object or fetish, known as the *djed*-column and thought to represent four pillars seen one behind the other, or a man's backbone, or most probably a Syrian cedar with its branches lopped off, was brought with them from Syria; after it they named their city Djedu. The city was subsequently renamed Per-Usire or Busiris after Usire, the Egyptian form of Osiris's name. The meaning of this name is uncertain, but it has been interpreted as 'to create a throne' and as Seat or Power of the Eye.

The Osiris fertility cult soon spread, apparently peacefully, to many other parts of Egypt. The god's associations with burial rites were also established early, for by the Fifth Dynasty he had absorbed the funerary gods of Abydos and dead pharaohs were identified with him. The funerary aspect was ultimately to become paramount and Osiris was to be considered the supreme god of Egypt. But in the beliefs about the 'First Time' Osiris was incorporated by mythology into the Heliopolitan Ennead, and it was easy to imagine this vegetation god to be the son of the earth-god Geb.

We have a fairly complete account of the Osiris myth in Plutarch's treatise, and its accuracy is attested to by confirmation of certain details in the *Pyramid Texts* and other documents of an early date. According to these, Nut gave birth to Osiris at Thebes on the first of the five intercalary days which Thoth created for Nut because he was in love with her. At the birth of Osiris a voice was heard in the temple crying that the great and good king was born, or that the lord of all was entering into light. Ra acknowledged Osiris as his heir, and in fact was sometimes said to have begotten both Osiris and Horus, Thoth having fathered Isis, and Geb only Set and Nephthys. It was also said that Osiris and Isis fell in love while still in the womb and there produced Horus the Elder. In any case they were married and Osiris succeeded to the throne of his father Geb.

Above. The divine mourners Isis and Nephthys protecting with their long wings the symbol of Osiris, the *djed*-column, here surmounted by the rising solar disk. The *djed* is thought to represent a tree-trunk with lopped branches, the tamarisk tree in which Osiris's body was enclosed until Isis could find it and bring it to life again. It was thus the most potent symbol of resurrection. Pectoral of Tutankhamon. Egyptian Museum, Cairo.

Opposite. Nut, spreading her feathery wings to welcome and protect the dead, just as she received the reborn sun each morning. The wings were borrowed from Isis and Nephthys, who as mourners and guardians of the dead took the form of kites. Like other pectorals from the tomb of Tutankhamon, this is in the shape of a shrine. Eighteenth Dynasty. Egyptian Museum, Cairo.

According to the Osiris legends, the people of the First Time were still barbarous cannibals; but Osiris instructed them in the ways of civilisation, teaching them what to eat, and showing them how to raise crops, including corn and vines. He taught them how to worship the gods and drew up laws for them. He was helped in his task by his scribe Thoth, who invented arts and sciences and gave names to things. Osiris ruled by power of persuasion, not by force; and he used the same methods when, having civilised Egypt, he decided to bring his teaching to the rest of the world. Leaving Isis as regent in his absence, Osiris set out on this mission accompanied by many musicians and minor gods. By argument and hymn-singing he persuaded the peoples he visited to follow the example of his own subjects, and taught them how to grow wheat, barley and vines, how to build cities and, in Ethiopia, how to regulate the flow of the Nile with irrigation canals and dams. During his absence Isis, assisted by Thoth, administered his kingdom, but she was hard pressed by the machinations of Set, who not only coveted the throne, but was also enamoured of her, and sought to change the established order.

Not long after the return of Osiris, Set, with the help of Aso, a queen of Ethiopia, and seventy-two conspirators, determined to do away with

Osiris. The details of this plot and of its sequel will be related later; but briefly, in the twenty-eighth year of his reign, on the seventeenth day of the month of Hathor (late September or November), Osiris fell to the conspirators and his body was cast by Set into the floodwaters of the Nile. Isis sought and found his body and with her own magic powers and the help of Thoth, Nephthys, Anubis and Horus, restored Osiris to life. But Osiris already belonged to the world of the dead, and though after his resurrection he could have reclaimed his throne, he preferred to maintain his kingdom in the land of the dead, leaving his vindication on earth in the hands of his posthumous son Horus.

This was one version of the Osiris myth. There seem, however, to have been many variants of the story. Perhaps more than in the case of any other god, the legend of Osiris underwent great changes through the course of history. In early times, certainly, he was a subsidiary god in the national religion; his myth did not at first belong to any of the great cosmogonic systems, but was subordinated to the family of gods venerated at Heliopolis, Hermopolis, Memphis and Thebes. The priests of those centres, anxious lest the ever-popular Osiris cult should swamp their own cults, accepted the fait accompli of gods combined into one human family by popular imagination. And it was the family setting of the Osiris myth that accounted for its widespread appeal. The suffering Osiris, head of an ideal family and model king, ultimately became the most important member of the divine family. As Osiris in this powerful and universal form does not properly belong to the early Egyptian religious systems, we shall leave a full consideration of the cult to a later section.

It seems that the form of the Osiris myth related above may derive from the reign of a real king, and certainly the peaceful dissemination of the benefits of civilisation in the myth corresponds to the unification of the Delta gods in the Osiris family and the peaceful spread of their worship as far as Abydos, thus unifying Lower

and Middle Egypt. The customary form of the story is rather different and will be recounted when we discuss Isis and Set. It is a far more complicated myth and explains why Osiris became universalised as a god of the dead and how he was able to become so particularly associated with the well-being of the royal house.

As god of the dead, Osiris enjoyed his greatest popularity; though he seems to have begun his mythic career as a rather frightening spirit of the Underworld, he ultimately came to represent for his devotees the hope of an eternally happy life in another world ruled over by a just and good king. This kingdom was supposed to be either beneath Nun, or in the northern heavens, or in the west, and was a gentle, fertile land.

Osiris retained his earliest associations with the fertility of the land and agriculture. The myths identified him with the cyclic pattern of birth, growth, death and renewal in the agricultural years; he was the source and the substance of corn, vines and trees. As the source of fertility, his death was associated with the dwindling Nile and his resurrection with its flood; the sun too, with its daily death and rebirth, became identified with Osiris. His rivalry with his brother Set was seen as the eternal opposition between the fertile Nile and the hostile desert, between life and death.

He was worshipped throughout Egypt, usually in a family triad with Isis and his posthumous son Horus. The chief centres of the cult were Busiris, his early home in the Delta, and Abydos, in Middle Egypt, the centre for the cult of the dead throughout recorded history and near Nedit, said to be where he was killed or where Isis found his body. Here Osiris was known as 'First of the Westerners', a title taken from the original god of Abydos, Khenti-Amentiu, and meaning King of the Dead. Beginning in the Old Kingdom, pharaohs were buried in Abydos, and later notables and others were buried there or had funerary stelas erected for them near the sanctuary. Eventually Egyptians

Above. Papyrus of Queen Nejmet, seen with her husband worshipping Osiris, and presenting him with gifts. In the upper panel are Isis and the four sons of Horus rising out of a lotus; in the lower panel the queen (*right*) is weighed against Mayet (*left*), the goddess of truth and justice who also forms the scales. Thoth as a dog-headed baboon records the verdict.

Right. Stela dedicated to the great triad of Horus, Osiris and Isis, who appear in the upper panel, with Titiaa, high priest of Amon, and his wife Aoui kneeling below to proffer gifts of fruit and flowers. Osiris wears the *atef* crown and carries the royal crook and flail, while his son Horus is represented not as Harpokrates but in his more usual form, like Horus the Elder – as a falcon-headed man. Musée du Louvre, Paris.

Opposite. A statue of the Roman period of Osiris, the last of the gods who reigned on earth as king, wearing the most majestic of the pharaoh's crowns, representing his power and glory as a warrior. Originally a pastoral god of the Delta, Osiris spread his cult by peaceful conquest. His chief cult centre was established at Abydos in Middle Egypt, with whose cult of the dead he became closely associated. Musei Vaticani.

On page 54. Isis holding a sistrum. Temple of Seti I at Abydos. This temple was completed and maintained by Seti's son Rameses II in return for Seti's intercession with the gods to grant Rameses a long reign. Nineteenth Dynasty.

all tried to make a pilgrimage to Abydos, in person or by proxy; and if not during their lifetime, then as part of their funerary ceremonies.

Osiris was represented as a dead king, with only the hands emerging from the mummy wrappings to grasp the emblems of his supreme power, the shepherd's crook and whip (sometimes called a flail for chastising the wicked). His body was coloured red for the earth or green for vegetation, and on his bearded head he wore the *atef* crown, composed of the white crown of Upper Egypt and the two red feathers of Busiris, to which were sometimes added the solar disk and a pair of horns. Osiris was generally seen as a passive figure, standing or seated on his throne, but he was also pictured at his resurrection, half-risen from his bier, and was represented by the *djed*-column and a box, said to contain his head.

Isis

Isis (or Eset) was also originally an independent and popular deity whose followers were established in predynastic times in the northern Delta, at Sebennytos. Like Osiris, and for the same reasons, Isis was brought mythologically into the Heliopolitan system. She too eventually absorbed deities of the Heliopolitan pantheon, and was ultimately to be identified or confused with all the goddesses as a great mother-goddess.

She was early said to be the wife of Osiris, god of the neighbouring western Delta, and her name, meaning 'seat' was taken to signify that she personified the throne of Osiris. Daughter of Geb and Nut and born on the fourth intercalary day, she was said to have borne Horus by union with Osiris either while still in the womb herself, or after the death of Osiris.

Isis was chiefly venerated for the part she played after the death of Osiris. Her role in the myth of Osiris during his reign on earth is small: we know simply that she married her brother, and helped him in his civilising mission by instituting marriage and teaching women the domestic arts of corn-grinding, flax-spinning

Above. A Nubian relief of Isis, one of the mightiest goddesses of the First Time, whose skills as Great Enchantress enabled her to extort the secret of his power from Ra. Here she carries the *ankh* and the papyrus sceptre of goddesses. She wears a feather dress and a headdress composed of a vulture, showing that she was identified with Mut, the horns and disk of Hathor and the hieroglyph for the name Isis, a seat.

On page 55. The deceased enthroned as Osiris, his hands emerging from mummy wrappings. A relief from one of the storage chambers in the Great Temple at Abu Simbel. The grandiose temples which Rameses II built at Abu Simbel not only absorbed a large proportion of the Nubian (Kushite) tribute: the contact their construction brought with the capital a thousand miles away helped consolidate the empire.

and weaving. According to some, however, as mother-goddess she taught Osiris the practice of agriculture. Her early character as the Great Enchantress was reflected in her magic powers and in her knowledge of the arts of medicine, which with the help of Thoth she taught mankind. During her husband's absence on his civilising mission, she governed Egypt wisely and kept close watch on her scheming brother Set.

Soon after the return of Osiris, Set invited him to a banquet at which he displayed a beautiful chest specially constructed to fit the king. As if for a joke, Set offered to give the chest to whichever guest could lie down in it. Several tried unsuccessfully, and then Osiris was persuaded to try. As soon as Osiris had climbed into it, Set and his fellow-conspirators closed the lid and nailed it down. They then weighted the chest with lead and cast it into the Nile.

When she heard the news, Isis put on widow's weeds, cut off half her hair and, weeping, set off to recover the chest and the body of her husband. She wandered through the land, asking everyone she met if they had seen the chest, and eventually came across some children who told her that they had seen it drifting towards the sea along the Tanitic branch of the Nile. Divine revelation now informed Isis that the chest had been carried across the sea to Byblos in Phoenicia where it had been washed ashore at the foot of a tamarisk tree. This tree had grown round the chest, enclosing it completely. The king of Byblos, Malacander, admiring the great size of the tree, had it cut down and used as a pillar in his palace.

Isis went to Byblos. The queen, Astarte, had recently given birth to a son and Isis made friends with her maids. The maids returned to the palace imbued with the heavenly scent of Isis, and Astarte, noticing this, asked for her to be summoned. She appointed Isis to be nurse to her newborn son.

Isis attempted to use her powers to confer immortality on the child, suckling it with only her finger and, at night, singeing it with a sacred and purifying flame in order to burn away the mortal quality of its body. But one day the queen surprised her new nurse, who in the form of a swallow was flying round and round the great tree. Her cries of alarm broke the spell and the chance of immortality for her son was irretrievably lost.

The goddess now revealed her true identity, and the king gave her the pillar. She immediately cut away the tamarisk and revealed the chest; she then fell upon it, wailing so loudly that the newborn child died at the sound. The king nevertheless provided Isis with a ship in which to return with the chest to Egypt, and sent his elder son to accompany her. As soon as she was embarked she opened the chest and gave vent to a fresh access of grief. The boy, wondering, approached her, but she turned on him with such fury that he died of fright – or according to some, fell backwards into the sea.

One reason for the violence of her grief was the fact that Isis had borne Osiris no son, so that there was no heir to the throne to defeat the purposes of Set. By her magic, however, Isis was able to conceive by her dead husband, some said while she was perched in the form of a kite mourning over his body.

On her return to Egypt, Isis hid in the Delta marshes near Buto, in order to conceal from Set both the recovery of Osiris's body and the fact that she was expecting a child. Set, however, discovered the coffer by chance while out hunting by moonlight in the marshes. He recognised the body of his dead brother, tore it into fourteen parts and scattered them throughout the kingdom.

Isis patiently began another search for her husband's body and, finding the parts one by one, preserved them carefully. At the place where each was found she held a funeral and set up a stela, hoping that Set would believe that the parts had really been buried in separate places. She found them all except the phallus, which Set had cast into the Nile, where it had been eaten by the Nile crab, which for this reason was accursed. But Isis modelled another and reconstituted the

An early mother and child theme in religion: Isis and the infant Horus, who is represented as an adult pharaoh. She wears on her head a disk set between the horns of a cow, representing the sistrum, a musical instrument usually carried by Hathor, with whom Isis was commonly identified. Such statues were generally portraits of the reigning queen – hence the *uraeus*. Musei Vaticani.

body of her husband, anointing it with precious oils. She thus performed the rites of embalmment for the first time, and thereby restored Osiris to eternal life, for it was always considered in Egypt that eternal life for the soul depended on the preservation intact of the physical body. She was assisted in her task by her sister Nephthys and, according to some versions, by Anubis, Thoth, Horus and even the four sons of Horus. (Such inconsistencies were of course due to later accretions and the growth in importance of Osirian beliefs.)

After she had recovered her husband's body and embalmed it, Isis was seized by Set and cast into prison. Set was angry at the funerary honours done to Osiris, but did not suspect that in fact his body had been made whole and resurrected. But with the aid of Osiris's vizier, Thoth, Isis managed to escape and so hide from Set the fact that she had conceived a child. Accompanied by seven protective serpents, she took refuge in the swamps of Buto and there gave birth to Horus. She rejoiced at having produced an heir for Osiris, and from then on lived for the day when he would be old enough to avenge his father and claim his patrimony, for there was no one to dispute Set's seizure of the throne.

Isis had no means of support for herself and the child, and was therefore forced to go out begging. One day, when she had been out all day, leaving the baby Horus hidden in the reeds, she came back to find him writhing about and half dead. Set, who was unable to enter the marshes in his real form, had taken the form of a poisonous snake and had crept up on Horus and bitten him. Isis was in despair, seemingly alone in the world: her father, her mother and her elder brother (Osiris) were dead; her younger brother (Set) was her implacable enemy and her sister Nephthys was his wife. Isis therefore appealed to all mankind. The marsh-dwellers and fishermen immediately came to offer their help and they wept in sympathy, but none of them knew a magical spell which would cure Horus of this poison. Isis guessed that the cause

of the evil was Set: the poisoning assumed cosmic proportions, representing the danger that the embodiment of innocence and goodness might be destroyed by the principle of evil and cunning.

This was the earliest manifestation of the great struggle between Horus and Set, which we shall meet again in the story of Horus. Isis now called upon the high god for aid. Her plea was heard in the 'Barque of Millions of Years', which when it drew level with her interrupted its course. Thoth descended from the boat to speak with Isis, and after expressing surprise that with her powers Isis was unable to set matters right, assured her that the power of Ra was at her disposal. When the sun's boat stopped the light stopped with it, and Thoth told Isis that the darkness would persist until Horus was cured.

Isis could hardly believe that Thoth was able on behalf of Ra to put things right, but she and Thoth realised the significance of the sun's stopping until Horus was cured: it meant that if Horus died, Ra's whole creation, the world, would be annihilated and Set, the principle of evil, would reign supreme; and Isis wished that she were

Horus herself, so that she should not have to see the consequences of his death. Thoth, however, reassured her, declaring that the magical protection enjoyed by Horus would henceforward be equal to that of the sun. Then, in the name of the sun, Thoth exorcised the poison from Horus's body, saying that the boat of Ra would stand still, that there would be no food, that the temples would be closed, that misery would never depart from the world, that eternal darkness would reign, that the wells would dry, that there would be no crops and no vegetation until Horus was cured.

This powerful spell of the sun-god Ra conquered the poison, and Isis and all the marsh-dwellers rejoiced. Thoth then recommended the child to their care, saying that he was now their responsibility on earth. Ra and Osiris would watch over him and Isis would spread his cult, and make him loved and respected. Finally, Thoth reported his success to Ra, saying that his *son* Horus had been saved.

This story, which touched the Egyptians deeply for its pathos, was also symbolic of the relation of the pharaoh to Ra and to the people.

Above. A section of the papyrus of Hent-Taui, a musician-priestess of Amon-Ra. The deceased is seen with Thoth, who revealed to the dead the magic formulae needed to traverse the underworld in safety. They are seen here adoring the sun-disk, which contains the Eye of Ra as it rises. Twenty-first Dynasty. British Museum, London.

Opposite. Isis owed her universal appeal to the human pathos of her sufferings as devoted wife and mother in the Osirian myths: all could identify with her as mourner. Her role in restoring Osiris and so ensuring the fertility of the land was vital and she became a saviour goddess in the Late Period. The drapery on her breast represents the *tat* or 'knot of Isis' – a fertility symbol. Musei Vaticani.

On page 58. Isis depicted at the foot of the sarcophagus of Amenhotep II, the position where she stood guard over the body of Osiris to ward off evil spirits. She wears a throne, the hieroglyph for her name, on her head and is kneeling on the emblem of gold, considered an agent of purification. Tomb of Amenhotep II, Valley of the Kings, Thebes.

On page 59. Isis, in the form of a bronze 'aegis'. As an ancient goddess of fertility who gradually absorbed other mother-goddesses of the Egyptian pantheon (here she wears the horns and the solar disk of Hathor) and as mistress of magic (spiritual power), Isis was far from being merely a defenceless, pathetic widow. The violence of her mourning could kill, her determination could resurrect, and she dared to challenge Ra himself. British Museum, London.

Horus was considered the archetype of the pharaohs, and the story's message was that Ra was supremely concerned with the welfare of his 'son', the pharaoh, and was able to protect him against all attacks by his enemies; but it was also the duty of the people to love and respect the pharaoh and as far as they could protect him. If the pharaoh should come to harm, the whole world order would collapse and the people themselves would necessarily die.

Against every other peril which assailed Horus while he lay hidden in the marshes of the Delta Isis was able to protect him. For, as we have already seen, she was skilled in the healing arts and had many spells at her command, having been instructed by Thoth. She often demonstrated how she could control Hike, magic, normally the companion and helper of Ra. It was told how, at a time when she was living on earth as a woman and was full of charm and persuasion, she tired of her existence among mankind and wished to be among the gods and stars. She wondered if she could not become sovereign over the earth and mistress of all the goddesses, and she hoped to extort this position from Ra by learning his secret name. Connected in the Egyptian mind with beliefs in magic incantations or spells was the idea that the knowledge of a person's name gave one power over that person – either because it revealed the key to his identity (indeed the person was inseparable from the name), or because it made it possible to recite spells against him.

Isis took advantage of the fact that Ra was now old and dribbled from the mouth. With the spittle that fell to the ground and the dust that adhered to it, she modelled a viper and placed it across Ra's daily path through the Two Lands. Next day, when Ra strode by, the viper bit him. The fire departed from Ra and he let forth a great cry which brought all the gods to his side. The mighty god could not cure himself of a wound inflicted by a creature he had not made, and none of Ra's children could help him.

Isis now approached him, seemingly innocent, and asked him solicitously what had happened. 'Has a snake poisoned you? Can it be that one of your own creatures has turned to strike at you? I shall conquer it with my spells! I shall make it recoil at the sight of your majesty!' Then Ra explained how he had been attacked by a serpent as he was making his usual daily journey, and told Isis what fearful pain he was in. 'It is not fire; it is not water. For I am colder than water and I am hotter than fire, and all my body sweats. I shiver and my eye trembles so that I cannot see the sky.' Isis replied, 'Tell me your name, divine father, for a man lives when his name is pronounced.' So Ra answered: 'I am the creator of the earth and of the mountains and of all that is upon the earth. I made the water and I made the sky and I placed the soul of the gods therein. When I open my eyes daylight appears, and when I shut them the night falls. At my command the mysterious waters of the Nile burst forth. I created the hours and the days. I give the signal for the festivals of the year and make the river. I am Khepri in the morning, Ra at midday and Atum in the evening.' But this did not cure Ra, for he still had not told his secret name.

Isis insisted that she could do nothing until he confided his real name. As soon as he told her this she would be able to cure him. At last Ra realised that there was no alternative but to give in to Isis. Therefore, hiding himself from the other gods, he caused the secret name to pass directly from his own bosom into that of Isis, at the same time forbidding her to reveal it to anyone other than her son Horus. Isis then called her son, telling him that Ra had promised to give up his two eyes to him, and only then did she exorcise the poison.

We may see in this myth, as in the myth of Isis and Horus in the marshes, an attempt to illustrate how the supreme power was transmitted to the Osirian triad, and in particular how the sun's power was communicated to Horus, or to his earthly counterpart, the pharaoh.

Isis maintained her cult over almost all periods of Egyptian history – indeed on the island of Philae in Upper Egypt she was worshipped until the sixth century A.D. She changed her aspect as Osiris did; and like him, she continued to be venerated simultaneously in her new aspects. Thus an important part of her worship was as a goddess of fertility. While Osiris represented the Nile floods, Isis symbolised the rich land of Egypt, which had to be protected from Set, the desert. As a sort of mother-goddess she absorbed the attributes of Hathor and Nut, Isis acquiring their solar mythology and iconography and the other goddesses becoming involved in funerary mythology.

Isis was, however, chiefly revered as the faithful wife and mourner. In this role she was often represented as a kite and accompanied by Nephthys, also as a kite, the two of them watching over the Canopic jars or perched at either end of a coffin. At other times she was seen protecting the deceased (Osiris or others identified with him) with long feathery wings. Most often Isis was represented as a woman with a throne on her head – the hieroglyph of her name. At other times her head-dress was a disk

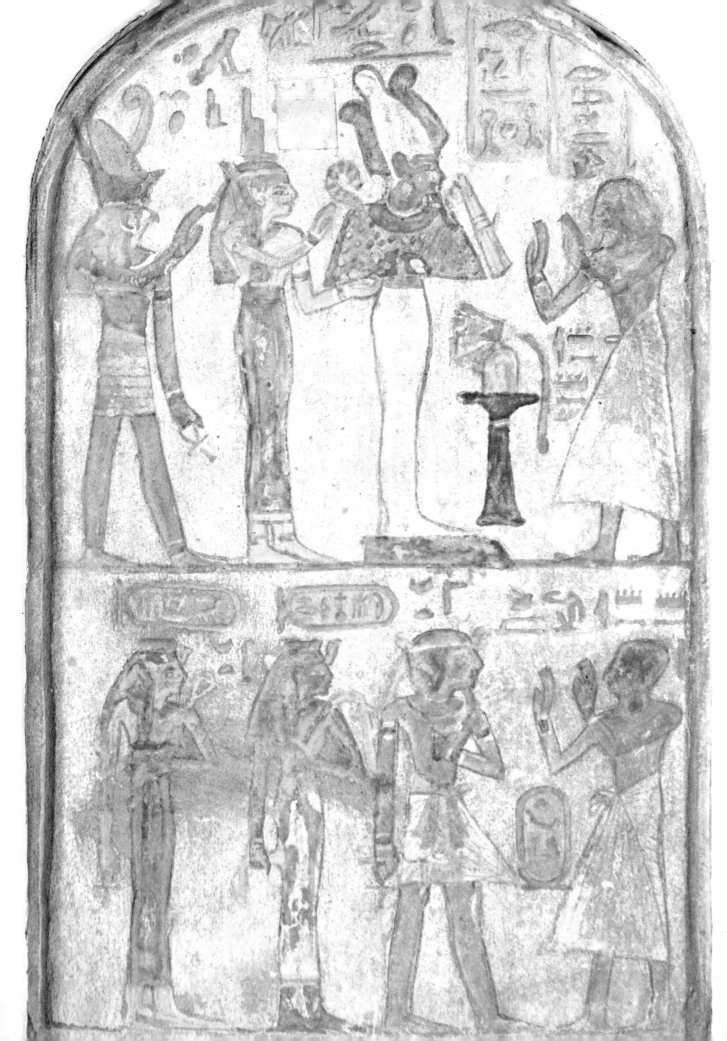

flanked by feathers and cow's horns; this derived from her identification with Hathor. She was sometimes shown with a cow's head; this, as we shall relate, was the head given her by Thoth when her own had been struck off by Horus in punishment for her thwarting his vengeance on Set. Sometimes Isis was shown as a woman with the crescent moon on her head, or crowned with lotus flowers and ears of corn, or bearing a cornucopia. In statues she was often shown suckling the infant Horus and she was revered as protectress of children, especially from disease. Her distinctive emblem was the *tat*, the 'girdle' or 'knot of Isis', which is thought to represent the generative powers.

Set

Set (or Seth or Sutekh) was another of the early deities, probably from Libya, whose followers seem to have worshipped him under crocodile and hippopotamus fetishes. Their capital was Nubt, later called Ombos, in Upper Egypt, though like the Horus-followers they were to some degree spread over the whole country. There seems to have been no great rivalry with the cults of Osiris and Isis, and as we have seen they were thought all to belong to the same family, Set having been born as the third child of Nut on the third intercalary day. He was married to his twin sister Nephthys. Later, the followers of Set must have resisted the southern followers of Horus who united the Two Lands under Menes, and this was mirrored in mythology by a feud.

With the advent of the followers of Ra, the Setians were evidently pushed back into Upper Egypt. The Ra-kings soon identified themselves with Horus. Meanwhile, however, the northern followers of Horus had been living in peace with their Delta neighbours, and their god had been integrated into the Osirian family as the son of Isis and Osiris. The feud therefore centred on an enmity between Set and his nephew Horus. Set justified his case by questioning the legitimacy of Horus – and indeed the Horus who was called the son of

Osiris was not really of the same family as the Horus who founded the First Dynasty.

The followers of Osiris blackened the character of Set from the moment of birth. They claimed that he was born neither at the right time nor in the right place, having torn himself from his mother's womb and burst through her side. He had red eyes and red hair, red being the colour of evil to the Egyptians. We have already outlined Plutarch's lengthy version of the myth of Osiris's reign, of Set's jealousy, and of his murder of his brother. It seems, however, that Plutarch omitted some details or misunderstood others. As we have seen elsewhere, Set's jealousy was not unfounded; for originally Geb had decreed that his kingdom should be divided between his sons, Upper Egypt going to Set, and Lower Egypt to Osiris. It was only after Set had protested at the partition, claiming the whole kingdom for himself, that he was denied any share at all in the patrimony. Or, according to another version, Osiris and Set began to rule according to Geb's partition, but Geb decided that Set was a bad ruler and gave his portion to Osiris. When Osiris then set out to conquer other lands, leaving Egypt in the hands of a woman, and when he furthermore used only peaceful means, Set as a warlike god inevitably felt aggrieved.

Set chose as his occasion for the attempt on his brother's life the festivals held at Memphis to celebrate Osiris's triumphal return, and it was here that he inveigled Osiris into the

chest which was to be his coffin, as recounted by Plutarch. Other accounts state that the murder took place at Nedit, near Abydos in Middle Egypt, and relate that Set simply seized Osiris and cast him into the Nile, whole or with his body cut into fourteen or sixteen parts. Some said that Isis and Nephthys found the body on the shores at Nedit; others agreed that the murder took place at Memphis, for they said that Isis and Nephthys saw it and buried the body at Memphis; yet others believed that the body was carried downstream by the floodwaters of the Nile and that it came to rest among the rushes or *byblus* of the Delta marshes, where Isis and Nephthys found it and resuscitated it. (*Byblus* was later misinterpreted as Byblos in Phoenicia.) But all agreed that when Isis took refuge in the Delta to bear and bring up her son Horus, Set sought her out and attempted to persecute her. And this again is not surprising, for Isis had come under the wing of Buto, who was not only a local goddess, but protective deity of the kingdom of Lower Egypt.

Set was of course associated with Upper Egypt even in the Osirian legend; and when we look at the evidence of earlier times, we find that he was known as Lord of Upper Egypt. His chief cult centre, Ombos, was near that of Nekhebet, protective goddess of Upper Egypt. In early dynastic times there seems to have been a relatively friendly division of Egypt between Set and Horus, the latter being known as Lord of Lower Egypt only. The pharaohs of the First and Second Dynasties looked to them both – Nubui, the 'two lords' – and they were sometimes represented as a man with two heads: one that of the Horus falcon and the other that of the Set animal. Set played an important part in coronation ritual and even in the Middle Kingdom he and Horus were shown together making the symbolic gestures of *samtaui*, or union of the Two Lands, by binding the plants of North and South around the emblem of union, which was the foundation of divine order.

Although Set still continued to be

thought a god, and was referred to as 'the Majesty of Set' – a style given to no other god than Ra – with the growth of the Horus cult and the position of Horus (the Elder) alone as inheritor of Ra, a great quarrel was imagined between them. During a fierce battle Horus castrated Set and Set as a black pig tore out Horus's weak eye, the moon; through this myth Set was sometimes identified with eclipses and the waning of the moon, which he was said to attack every month because it contained the soul of Osiris. But sight was restored to Horus and a tribunal of the gods awarded him the entire kingdom. When the Horus and Osiris myths became entwined the enmity was transferred to Horus son of Osiris, and Set became the murderer of Osiris.

The tribunal of the gods gave judgement in favour of Horus; but Ra as its president consistently upheld the claims of Set, for when Horus was considered the son of Ra, Set was also thought to be his son. Ra was in fact dependent on Set: as a warlike god he was one of the most important of those who stood in the solar barque in order to defend Ra against his enemies, especially his most implacable and dangerous foe, the serpent Apep

or Apophis. During the trial to decide between Horus and Set, Set boasted of his prowess in daily defending Ra, and claimed that on account of his great strength he should be awarded the kingdom. But the *Book of the Dead* described how Set was not content merely to have the honour of defending the chief of the gods. There was more braggadocio about him than real courage, and having slain Apep, partly by ruse, he then turned to Ra to proclaim his triumph and to demand that Ra should recognise how brave he was. He told Ra tauntingly that he could come out of hiding now that Apep was dead, bringing with him all his paraphernalia (his divine symbols of power). Finally Set warned Ra to treat him well or he would raise his storms and thunder against him. At this Ra ordered his crew to chase Set away, which they did, Nut calling Set a windbag. Then, freed from disturbance, Ra made his divine dawn appearance.

This myth combined the two aspects of Set. His presence in his good aspect as the slayer of Apep was essential to the safe passage of Ra on his daily voyage; but it was equally essential that he should be banished from the boat before the divine party

could proceed. The last requirement no doubt explains why Set was rarely depicted in representations of the solar barque, his place being taken by Thoth. In the same way, in one variant of the myth, Set was punished by being made to bear Osiris on his shoulders or to provide a gentle breeze to bear Osiris's boat along – a humbling but useful service. In another version Set was exiled to the sky where, as a 'consolation' for his loss of the throne, he was embodied in the Great Bear and allowed to make as much noise as he wished as god of winds and storm. Most commonly, having lost even his relatively infertile southern kingdom, Set was relegated to the desert borders as the personification of aridity and god of foreigners.

This last identification was facilitated by his rise to power under the foreign Hyksos pharaohs of the Fifteenth Dynasty, who connected him with their own Mesopotamian god Sutekh. The only other period in which Set regained favour was in the Nineteenth Dynasty when some of the Rameses pharaohs, wishing to emulate the military prowess of the Hyksos, gave themselves names such as 'beloved of Set'. This revival was

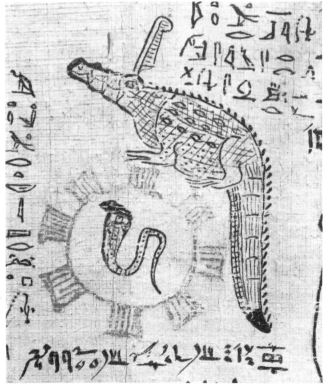

Above. The serpent Apep, Ra's eternal foe, was a malevolent figure and an enemy of the dead. Here the deceased with the help of his three sons attempts to placate Apep, who also attacked the souls of the dead in the Underworld. British Museum, London.

Opposite right. Detail from a magical papyrus which was a guide for the owner on his journey through the underworld. The crocodile was the emblem of Sebek, worshipped in the Faiyum and at Ombos. Though Set took the form of a crocodile, the creature was commonly thought to have helped reconstitute the body of Osiris and was worshipped accordingly. British Museum, London.

Opposite left. Horus and Set (with the head of the Typhonian animal) symbolise the union of the Two Lands by the ritual gesture of *samtaui*, in which they bind the heraldic plants of Upper and Lower Egypt round the symbol of union, the basis of Egypt's well-being and the power of the pharaoh, whose cartouche it forms.

short-lived: thereafter Osirianism permanently gained the upper hand, and Set was increasingly degraded, until by the Twenty-sixth Dynasty he became the personification of evil and was actually identified with his ancient foe Apep. In the Twenty-second Dynasty many representations of Set, including references to him on monuments, were effaced or replaced by images of Thoth or Sebek, the crocodile-god.

Set was represented by the so-called Typhonian animal, or wore its head on human shoulders. This strange animal with its long curving snout, square upstanding ears and upright tufted tail has not been identified, though some think it might be a wild pig, the form in which Set on one occasion attacked Horus. Desert animals, pigs and boars, hippopo-

tami, crocodiles and serpents were associated with Set.

Nephthys

Nephthys was Nut's second daughter and was born on the fifth intercalary day. Though she was married to Set, her loyalties were with Osiris, and indeed her name, Nebhet, meant 'Lady of the House' and is thought to refer to the Palace of Osiris. As wife of the god of aridity and storm, Nephthys conceived no children. Her greatest wish was to have a child by Osiris, so she either made him drunk or disguised herself as Isis in order to deceive him. The fruit of their union was Anubis; but for fear of Set's vengeance Nephthys exposed the infant as soon as he was born. Soon afterwards Set murdered Osiris and

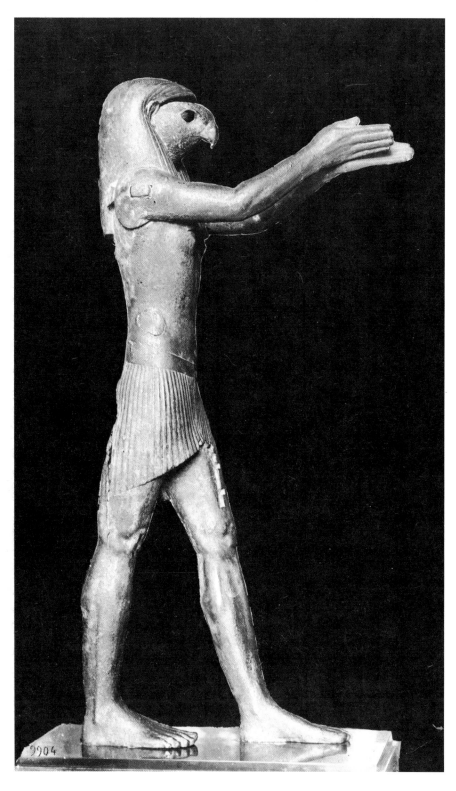

with Osiris, 'Nephthys' mourned at the head of the coffin, while 'Isis' stood or perched at the foot. Like Isis, she enfolded and protected the deceased with her long feathery wings and was often represented thus on coffins. She was said to be the friend of the dead in the judgement hall of Osiris.

Horus

The name Horus is the Latinised form of the Egyptian Hor, which seems to mean 'face', and was applied to the falcon-god of early invaders of the Nile valley. The falcon-deity was at first a sky-god, the sun and moon being his eyes, and this might explain the name Hor. From being the emblem of a conquering people, the falcon came to symbolise a warrior-god and victorious leader. Consideration of his pre-eminence in turn led to the belief that the king was his earthly embodiment. This belief later hardened into dogma and the kings took the name of Horus as one of their own. At the same time, the ruling kings were now followers of Ra, so Horus became identified with the sun. Meanwhile, however, he had become identified in the popular mind (as opposed to the state religion) as the son of Osiris.

Nephthys fled from her husband. She joined Isis in the search for the body of Osiris and told her sister about Anubis. Isis was able to find the baby during the search for Osiris in the Delta marshes, and adopted him.

Nephthys thereafter joined Isis in all her trials, Isis protecting her – and others who had fled in horror from Set – by applying her magic powers of transformation to them so that they were able to hide in the form of various animals. Having found the body of Osiris, the two sisters together embalmed it; then, as kites, Isis and Nephthys mourned over the corpse. In the same way, in funerary rites when the deceased was identified

The interaction of these two identifications was the most fertile source of myth-making for, though in many aspects the two Horuses are quite distinct, in later times the Egyptians confused the solar Horus and the Osirian god of the same name. Resolutions of the confusion differed in the various cult centres, and so at least fifteen important Horus gods can be distinguished. However confused, these forms can be roughly divided into solar and Osirian according to the parentage ascribed to Horus in the myth. Those in which Horus was the son of Atum, or of Ra, or of Geb and Nut are solar; while those in which Horus was the son of Isis are Osirian. We shall consider first the solar forms of Horus.

Haroeris

Haroeris (or Harwer), one of the earliest forms of Horus, derived from the combination of the falcon-god with an indigenous deity Wer, 'the Great One', a god of light whose eyes

were the sun and the moon. Though increasing emphasis was put on the right eye, the sun, Haroeris was worshipped as Mekhenti-irty, 'He on whose brow are the Two Eyes' or, on moonless nights, as Mekhenti-en-irty, 'He on whose brow there are not eyes' – in which aspect he was patron of the blind. Mekhenti-irty or Hormerti was represented holding in his hands the two *udjat* or *uraeus* eyes of Horus.

Haroeris, or Horus the Elder, was said to be the son, or sometimes the husband of Hathor. He was also the brother of Osiris and Set. We have already referred to his great fight with Set over the succession in which his eyes were torn out; this myth was carried over in various forms to Horus son of Osiris, in which versions Horus handed one of the eyes to Osiris as a token of life, taking back only one eye for himself. Horus then ascended the throne, justified by the tribunal of gods. Thus myth allowed Horus of Two Eyes to give way to Hor Nubti 'Horus Vanquisher of Set' or Horus of Ombos (Set's cult centre) and to other forms of the falcon-god in which Horus was identified with Ra.

Horus Behdety

Horus Behdety was the form of Horus the Elder worshipped in the western Delta at Behdet. When his followers spread into Upper Egypt and established the cult centre at Edfu this became known as the Behdet of Upper Egypt, also called Hierakonpolis. As son and heir of Ra, Behdety was a form of Horus assimilated to the Heliopolitan system but not yet completely identified with Ra. The Egyptians explained the connection of Horus with Edfu as follows:

In the reign of Ra not as sun-god but as earthly king of Upper and Lower Egypt, the royal army was in Nubia when the King was informed that there was a plot against him in Egypt. The plotters seem to have been aided by malignant powers, or perhaps to have been some kind of demons, and their leader was Set. The King sailed downstream and, landing at Edfu, ordered his son Horus to

Above. Bas-relief showing a scarab and one of the rare ram-headed representations of Harmakhis, the rising sun, who was associated with the Khepri scarab in the symbolism of eternal life. From the tomb of Seti I, father of Rameses II. Nineteenth Dynasty.

Opposite. Column with relief of Rameses II, wearing a warrior's crown and carrying lotus flowers. Above his head hovers a Horus falcon, the pharaohs' protective divinity. In its claws it holds the symbol for the course of the heavenly bodies, which represented eternity and also formed the outline of the royal cartouche. Eighteenth Dynasty.

fight the enemy. Horus flew up into the sky, taking the form of a winged sun-disk and, seeing the enemy, flew down to the attack. He inflicted such damage on them that they fled. As a reward for his prowess, the King, when he heard of this rout, bestowed upon his son the title Horus of Edfu.

The enemy were, however, not yet defeated, for they changed themselves into crocodiles and hippopotami and attacked the boat of Ra himself. Again, Horus and his followers routed them, harpooning them from the boat. Once more assuming the form of a winged sun-disk and setting himself at the prow of the boat, Horus pursued the survivors throughout Upper and Lower Egypt, inflicting terrible defeats upon them. He beheaded Set in front of Ra and dragged him by the feet through Egypt.

In the second part of this story, the

characters changed somewhat, for Horus, son of Ra, became confused with Horus, son of Osiris. The leader of the enemy was now Set, reborn and the enemy of Osiris. Set took the form of a serpent and the fighting continued throughout Lower Egypt as far as the frontiers of Asia. Horus, who took the form of a falcon-headed staff with a triangular spear-point, was, however, victorious. To seal his victory, he again sailed upstream to Upper Egypt and put down another rebellion. As a reward for this triumph, Ra decreed that the winged sun-disk should be placed on all temples and shrines of all deities in order to ward off enemies.

Horus Behdety was therefore most frequently represented as a winged sun-disk sculpted over the gates of sanctuaries. Alternatively he was shown as a falcon hovering over the pharaoh in battle scenes, his claws grasping the whisk or flail of royalty and the ring of eternity. He also appeared as a man with a falcon's head wearing the double crown. One of his symbols was the falcon-headed staff, the instrument of Set's destruction. When bearing it he was shown as a hawk-headed man. The bas-reliefs in his Edfu temple showed him leading the forces of Ra-Harakhte against Set. As it was always the god himself who led his forces into battle, Horus was already plainly considered indistinguishable from Ra.

Harakhte

Harakhte, whose name meant 'Horus of the Horizon', and who was also called 'Horus of the Two Horizons', was the form which Horus took when his early characteristics as a god of light were emphasised. He was identified with Ra as he made his daily journey from the eastern to the western horizon, and especially with his Khepri and Atum aspects. The roles of the two gods as solar and as royal deities became inextricably mixed, and under their combined authority Ra-Harakhte held sway over all Egypt. He was represented as a falcon or a falcon-headed man wearing the solar disk and triple crown or the *uraeus* and the *atef* crown.

Harmakhis

Harmakhis, 'Horus in the Horizon', personified the rising sun and was associated with Khepri as symbol of resurrection or eternal life. Though sometimes represented as a falcon-headed man wearing a variety of crowns and sometimes as a falcon-headed lion, or as a ram-headed lion, his most famous representation was as the Sphinx of Giza, a vast man-headed lion wearing the royal head-dress and the *uraeus*. This was sculpted out of the living rock near the tomb of Khephren, a pharaoh of the Fourth Dynasty, the face being in his image; sphinxes were usually identified with the pharaoh in his immortal aspect.

Harmakhis was considered to be not only the sun-god as Horus, but also the repository of the deepest wisdom. Thuthmosis III in the Eighteenth Dynasty told how, when he was a young prince out hunting, he chanced to fall asleep at noon in the shadow between the great paws of

Harmakhis of Giza. In his dream he heard a voice saying: 'Behold me, my son Thuthmosis. I am thy father Harmakhis-Atum-Khepri. Thou shalt assume the white crown and the red crown upon the Throne of Geb.' The god went on to explain that he would obtain the throne for Thuthmosis provided he in return would remove the sand which over the centuries had half buried the sphinx. Thuthmosis rendered this service to Harmakhis and in due course became the pharaoh – under the protection of Ra-Harmakhis rather than Amon-Ra. Thus began the movement against Amon-Ra that was to culminate in Atenism.

Harsiesis

Harsiesis, whose name meant 'Horus son of Isis', was specifically the Osirian deity, though with the growth in popularity of Osirianism he absorbed some of the functions of the solar Horus. As we have seen, he was conceived by Isis magically after the

death of Osiris and brought up by her secretly on the floating island of Chemmis in the marshes near Buto. The child was weak at birth and a constant prey to the machinations of his wicked uncle Set, who sent all manner of serpents and diseases to attack him. But his mother, the Great Enchantress, was able to shield him from these emanations of evil by means of her spell against creatures biting with their mouths and stinging with their tails, and Horus survived. As a child he was known as Harpokrates, 'the infant Horus', and was often represented as a baby being suckled by Isis. He was said to be stunted from the waist down, perhaps because his father was dead when he was conceived, and perhaps because he was born prematurely. This may be why he was usually represented seated as a child and sucking his thumb, his head shaved except for the sidelock of youth falling to his shoulder. Even in this form, however, he wore the royal crown and *uraeus*,

Opposite. Bronze figure of Harpokrates, 'the infant Horus', here seen wearing the double-crown or *pschent* of the pharaohs, who identified themselves with him. Usually represented as an infant with his finger to his lips and with the sidelock of youth. Nineteenth Dynasty. British Museum, London.

Below. Head of the sphinx at Giza. Constructed from a single piece of rock in the reign of Khephren (c. 2650 B.C.) and probably fashioned in his likeness. The pharaoh, the living Horus, was usually the model for sphinxes, representations of Harmakhis.

and in later times was identified with the newborn sun, and represented with the solar disk and plumes.

While Horus was growing up at Buto, Osiris returned frequently from the shades in order to instruct him in the art of warfare. Horus grew up believing that the finest thing possible was to avenge one's father and mother when they have been ill-treated. At last he grew to manhood and was ready to make war on Set, to see justice done, and to regain the throne of his father. Many of the other deities joined his ranks. But it was his own deeds of valour in the long war which now opened that won for him the title Harendotes, 'Horus avenger of his father'.

The battles with Set earlier attributed to Behdety were considered to be the opening campaign of Harsiesis. Horus showed great military skill, and succeeded in piercing Set with his lance and even in striking off his head and bringing it to Isis. But despite his repeated success in cutting Set's forces

to pieces, he was unable to overcome his adversary, who was always able to recover from his wounds. Besides, Set was a warrior-god par excellence while Horus was still a stripling, brave but unable to counter the machinations of his uncle.

The war dragged on and Set thought that he could gain some advantage through bringing the matter to arbitration by a tribunal of the gods. First he had Osiris summoned before it; but Thoth was so able an advocate that the gods declared in favour of Osiris, who was found to be 'true of voice'. Set, however, could not accept that Horus should ascend the throne, and had him too brought before the court. This trial was the subject of one of the few consecutive stories connected with Egyptian mythology that have survived.

The court could not make a decision either way, for its members, presided over by Ra-Harakhte, seemed always to agree with the last speaker brought to testify before them, and they constantly changed their minds. After the trial had already lasted for eighty years, they were all heartily bored with it and totally unable to resolve their differences. Most of the tribunal favoured Horus, who against Set's accusations that his nephew was a bastard, only the alleged son of Osiris, had established the legitimacy of his birth; but the president, Ra-Harakhte, favoured Set because he was the son of Nut.

Though he had fought a lengthy war with Set and had been before the tribunal for eighty years, Horus was still represented as little more than a child. Set, according to Ra-Harakhte, was the older and more experienced and therefore the better fitted to be the ruler of Egypt; Horus, who claimed the throne by right of succession, was too young to govern. In symbolic terms, therefore, the great struggle between Horus and Set represented differences of opinion about what reasons a man may adduce in claiming rights over property. While Horus claimed by right of succession, Set boasted that he was the strongest in the Great Ennead (i.e. stronger than Ra-Harakhte himself), for every

day he killed Apep, the chief enemy of the sun-god. Horus had no defence but the law of succession and the justice of the gods.

After eighty years of wrangling, however, Shu and Thoth recommended Horus's case to the tribunal on the grounds that justice should prevail over brute strength; Isis immediately assumed that the issue was settled and she declared that the will of the tribunal was that the Eye

(symbol of royal power) should be presented to Horus. But Ra-Harakhte was offended that the conduct of the tribunal had been snatched away from him in this way and, furious, stopped the gods from presenting the Eye to Horus. Set, now regretting that he had brought the matter before the court and unsure of his moral justification, suggested trial by combat; but Thoth opposed this on the grounds that it would be to avoid the vital decision as to who was in the right. The tribunal was once more in deadlock.

The gods decided to summon the ram-god of Mendes, who came before them together with Ptah of the primeval mound. But neither of them was prepared to give judgement, merely suggesting that the tribunal should write for guidance to Neith, goddess of Sais, the oldest of the goddesses. Thoth was instructed to write a formal letter requesting her views. Neith, like the other deities, favoured Horus. She replied that the throne should be given to Horus, while Set should receive compensation in the form of twice his existing property and two more wives, Astarte and Anat, who were Syrian goddesses. The gods of the tribunal once more thought that a solution had at last been reached and cried out that Neith was right. Once more, however, Ra-Harakhte resented their haste, and reproached Horus with his youth. Tempers among the gods were by now short and one of them, Baba, seeing that only Ra-Harakhte's obstinacy was keeping them, called out to him: 'Your shrine is empty!'

Mortally offended at this insult, Ra-Harakhte lay down on his back and sulked. The tribunal broke up. Only Hathor was able to persuade him to rejoin the tribunal; she went to her father's house and, showing him her private parts, so cheered him up that he forgot his displeasure!

After the tribunal had been reconvened, arguments again hinged on the two methods of determining the disputants' qualification: by ability or by patrilineal succession. As each case was put, the gods applauded it and they got no further.

Isis, whom Set had had excluded from the tribunal, eventually bribed Anty, the ferryman of the gods, to take her to the Middle Island, to which the court had shifted. Always a powerful sorceress, Isis then transformed herself into a ravishing young maiden; Set saw her from where he was seated with the other gods and went secretly to waylay her. When he spoke to her she told him a story of how her husband, a shepherd, had died leaving her with a little boy who looked after his father's cattle. Then a stranger had come up to the son and said: 'I shall beat you, take your father's cattle and chase you away.' Isis then asked Set if he would help her son against this stranger. Set, hoping to please the beautiful maiden, answered: 'Should cattle be given to strangers when a man has a son as heir?' Thereupon Isis turned into a kite, flew up to a treetop, and called to Set that he had condemned himself out of his own mouth.

Set, overwhelmed at the injustice of this trickery, went weeping to complain to Ra-Harakhte. But the president of the tribunal could only agree with Isis, that Set had condemned himself.

Ra-Harakhte now became impatient to end the dispute and instructed the gods, who had sat down idly on a mountainside, that they should immediately place the crown on Horus's head. But Set would not accept this judgement. He proposed, and the

Right. The goddess Neith, wearing the red crown of Lower Egypt. She was an ancient local deity of Sais in the Delta and became associated with Osirianism as one of the guardians of coffins and Canopic jars. In the Late Period she was regarded as a universal mother and said to be the wife of Khnum. Twenty-sixth (Saite) Dynasty. Ägyptisches Museum, East Berlin.

Opposite. Osiris, though god of the dead, was also provider of fertility and prosperity to the living. In this benign-looking wooden statuette, he wears the *atef* crown, composed of the white crown of Upper Egypt and the red feathers of Busiris in the Delta, and clasps his shepherd's crook and whip. Musée du Louvre, Paris.

Below. Bronze seated figure of Ra, the great sun-god, with the solar disk on his head and a papyrus sceptre. Twenty-second Dynasty. British Museum, London.

gods agreed, that he and Horus should decide the issue by turning themselves into hippopotami and diving into the water. Whichever of them left the water before the end of three months should be declared the loser. Isis was in despair, for the hippopotamus was a form natural to Set and she was sure that he would kill Horus. So she fixed a harpoon to a length of rope and cast it into the water. It first pierced Horus; she released him hastily when she heard his cries. Her next cast was more fortunate and caught Set – but he at once cried out to her, as his sister and in memory of their common mother, to release him likewise. Isis, sentimentally moved by this plea, released him, whereupon Horus, enraged by this weakness, sprang out of the water and cut off his mother's head.

The gods resolved to punish Horus for this crime, but he had gone into hiding on a mountain and could not be found. Set, however, managed to track him down and tore out his eyes, which he buried in the soil of the mountain; lotus flowers, the symbol of rebirth and of the sun, grew out of them. Set then returned to the gods and declared that he had been unable to find Horus.

But he was found, by Hathor (in some versions it is Thoth), lying on the mountainside. She took gazelle's milk and by rubbing it into his eye-sockets, restored his sight. Together they returned to the company of the gods.

The struggle was at once renewed and every weapon was used: calumny, trickery, and force. Set even attempted a sexual assault, knowing that it would expose Horus to contempt if it succeeded. But this was foiled by the watchful Isis and turned against Set, as we shall see. Horus himself was not above using trickery; Set proposed that they should sail about in boats cut out of stone, and whoever should sink the other's boat first should inherit the throne of Osiris; Horus agreed but in fact made his boat of cedar-wood covered with plaster. Set was deceived and they pushed out from the shore. Set's stone boat immediately sank and he attempted to escape by turning himself into a hippopotamus, but Horus gave chase and inflicted terrible wounds on him with his harpoon. Horus was often represented spearing a hippopotamus in the neck and binding it with chains. Nevertheless Set again escaped.

A decision still could not be reached. Neith was again approached, but again without success. Eventually, and decisively, it was agreed on the advice of Thoth to appeal to Osiris for final judgement.

Osiris naturally replied in favour of his son, reproaching the gods for delaying the judgement for so long and for ill-treating Horus. Was Osiris not the god whom they had to thank for their barley and spelt and cattle? No other god performed such services. Ra-Harakhte, angered at this assertion, retorted that even if Osiris had never existed there would still be barley and spelt.

Osiris's reply to this curt letter settled the dispute, and defined the spheres of power of the god of the living and the god of the dead. Osiris praised the supreme god of the Ennead for all that he had done, including the establishment of the halls of judgement in the Underworld. But he added that Mayet had been cast down. Osiris did not veil his threat: he spoke of the 'savage-faced messengers' which he had at his disposal, whom he could send to fetch the heart of any god or mortal who performed evil deeds. It was ordained that every being – gods and stars, nobles and common people – should pass into the West, the land of the dead. There they should be subject to the judgement of Osiris, who was thus ultimately the lord of all of them.

Backed by this threat, the judgement of Osiris in favour of his son was accepted by the tribunal. Set's pride, however, still did not allow him to accept legal judgement rather than judgement through force of arms. He was brought in chains before the gods, who spared his life on condition that, as god of storms and the wind, he would convey the boat of Osiris.

Horus's heritage was now restored to him and he was declared ruler of the two Egypts and given the title Har-pa-Neb-Taui, 'Horus Lord of the Two Lands'. Horus re-established the reign of Mayet, divinely ordered justice, throughout the land, rebuilding the temples of his ancestors which had been destroyed under Set, and building new ones in commemoration of his struggles with Set and of the victory of justice. His reign was the model for all pharaohs thereafter, each of whom took the title 'Living Horus'. Though Horus retained close links with both the solar and the Osirian systems, by combining his roles he transcended both of them.

Thus Ra was no longer a rival as a dynastic god, for he was relegated to heaven, with Horus forming the principal link with heaven, the ladder of the sky; and Osiris remained in the afterworld, with men dependent on Horus for safe passage through the hall of judgement, for Horus led the deceased into the presence of Osiris and often supervised the weighing of the heart. Horus the Child became as it were a further generation, for he was identified with the heir to the throne who would eventually avenge or 'justify' his father.

Horus was generally thought to be married to Hathor, though he had other wives as well. She bore him a number of children, the most important of which were Ihy, god of music; and Harsomtus, 'uniter of the Two Lands', whose cult centre was Dendera and who was represented as a human-headed mummy, a serpent-headed man, or a falcon-headed man with plumes and disk. Often Horus himself was called Harsomtus. His best-known sons, however, were the four who presided over the Canopic jars and who had helped him in devising the funerary rites for Osiris; he was said to have had these sons by his mother Isis.

Horus was universally worshipped, not only in the person of the pharaoh (never in fact a very popular cult), but wherever Isis and Osiris were venerated. He was also a member of other triads, especially with Hathor, and in late times, with the rise of Isis as great mother-goddess, he was much worshipped in his form of Harpokrates.

Hathor

Hathor was a great sky-goddess who was represented as a cow and became known as a universal mother-goddess, sometimes being called creator of the universe. Her name, which seems to mean 'House of the Face', probably referred to the early fetish from which her cult grew. This was a cow's face, which was later likened to a sistrum. Hathor remained one of the few deities who was represented full-face. The name of Horus derived from the same root, and so Hathor became closely associated with him.

Above. Sekhmet, the lion-headed Eye of Ra, goddess of the scorching, destructive power of the sun and defender of the divine order. She was considered the wife of Ptah in the Memphite triad, and the daughter of Ra.

Opposite. Limestone stela of Upuaut–mes, showing the deceased worshipping the gods Ra-Harakhte (*right*) and Osiris (*left*) c. 1300 B.C. (Nineteenth Dynasty). Despite the rise of Osirianism, the deceased still sought to justify himself before the ancient judge of the dead. Ägyptisches Museum, East Berlin.

Above. Horus supervising the weighing of the heart in the hall of judgement. Anubis can be seen on the left verifying the balance of the deceased's heart in one pan of the scales against Truth in the other. The result is recorded by Thoth in his ibis-headed form, as scribe of the gods. Painted funerary casket of the Twentieth Dynasty. Musée du Louvre, Paris.

Opposite. A detail from the figure of Hathor, as a cow, giving milk to the young Amenhotep II. As Hathor was drawn into Osirian mythology, she was increasingly pictured as suckling the dead, as well as the living Horus. The spots on her body represent stars, the souls of the dead. Eighteenth Dynasty.

Above. Bronze mirror with handle fashioned in the form of a papyrus sceptre and the head of the goddess Hathor, her broad face flanked by cow's ears and horns. Hathor presided at the toilet of women. c. 1500 B.C. Ägyptisches Museum, East Berlin.

Opposite. Limestone relief of the goddess of joy, Hathor, from the funerary temple near Saqqara of King Sahure, one of the three pharaohs of the Fifth Dynasty who were the first to claim physical descent from Ra by the wife of a priest of Ra. Their fine temples and pyramids were dedicated to the sun-god. Part of a procession of gods bearing pharaonic sacrifices. Early Fifth Dynasty.

At first, however, Hathor was thought to be the daughter of Nut and Ra. Like Nut, she was a cow; and from being the beloved daughter of Ra, she came to be considered his wife. By union with the Bull of Ra she bore her son Ihy, who was known as god of music and wore the royal double crown and sidelock of youth. Hathor was also known as the Eye of Ra, for the Eye took the form of Hathor when Ra sent it to subdue his rebellious subjects during his reign on earth. The mighty Hathor soon put fear in men's hearts; she returned after the first day as mighty as a lion, declaring that her heart rejoiced, for she imposed her will upon men. In her fury Hathor embodied herself in the lioness-deity Sekhmet who, having tasted blood, could not be appeased. Ra wished to rule mankind, not to destroy it utterly; but the only way he could now control his bloodthirsty daughter was to deceive her. Accordingly he ordered his servants to brew great quantities of beer and to colour it with red berries; this was spread across the fields in the night and next morning, when Hathor set out to demolish mankind, she paused to admire the 'blood' and to drink it. Soon she became drunk and abandoned her project, reverting to her usual character.

This character was quite the reverse of Sekhmet's, for normally Hathor was the goddess of joy and motherhood, the embodiment of all that is best in women. Like Nut, with whom she was often confused, she was said to be the mother of Horus the Elder by Ra. But she was even more generally thought of as the wife of Horus of Edfu (one of the forms of Horus the Elder), her name being interpreted to mean 'House of Horus'. Their sacred marriage was celebrated annually when the image of Hathor was taken from Dendera to the shrine of Horus at Edfu. The fruit of their union was said to be Horus the Younger. This is why Isis was so often depicted with cow's horns when venerated as the mother of Horus. When Hathor was not actually said to be the mother of Horus the Younger, it was customary for her to be depicted as his nurse.

In the same way Hathor was said to suckle the pharaoh, the living Horus. When she was considered in this aspect it was natural to identify the queen with Hathor. The queen as chief priestess led the other priestesses, the concubines of the god, in the dancing and music-making which were their part in the temple ritual of Horus and the other gods. The lesser priestesses were identified with the Seven Hathors, while Hathor was considered the goddess of music and dancing. In this aspect her emblem was the sistrum, the instrument carried by her son Ihy. She was also the goddess of light-hearted pleasure and

Hathor was represented as a star-spangled cow, as a woman with a cow's head, or as a woman with a broad human or sistrum-shaped head and cow's ears or wearing a solar disk between horns. She is most often seen with a sistrum as goddess of joy; suckling the living or the dead; or as goddess of the West, standing on the mountain of the West to welcome the dying sun into her arms – a combination of her solar and Osirian characters.

Anubis

Anubis was a dog- or jackal-deity whose cult seems to have originated at Thinis near Abydos, but spread early to most parts of Egypt. The jackal being a desert animal, the Egyptians associated Anubis with the western desert, the home of the dead. He took over the title of the funerary god Khenti-Amentiu, 'First of the Westerners', but this was in turn usurped by Osiris.

It seems that at first Anubis was the god of death for the pharaoh alone. It is thought that in early times the pharaoh may have been ritually put to death by viper poisoning at the end of twenty-eight years' reign. When the end came Anubis (or a priest representing him) would appear to the pharaoh with a viper. Though this practice was ended, Anubis remained the announcer of death, and was represented as a warrior bearing daggers and a coiled viper or cobra. It is interesting in this connection that Osiris was murdered after twenty-eight years on the throne.

As he could foresee a mortal's destiny, Anubis was associated with magic and divination. He was depicted at the bottom of divination bowls, so that the seer saw Anubis first, leading the other gods who would come to reveal the secrets of the future.

When Anubis became identified with the Osirian afterworld he was said to be the son of Nephthys by Osiris. We have seen how Nephthys deceived Osiris into giving her this son, and how Isis saved his life by finding him after Osiris's death, being led to him by dogs. Isis adopted the

of love. She presided over the toilet of women, all of whom worshipped her – from the queen to the lowliest woman of the land – and she was considered the protectress of pregnant women and a sort of midwife. Her connections with fertility naturally led to her association with the rise of the Nile and the Dog-star Sothis, when she was represented lying in a ship as a cow with a star between her horns.

Her role changed somewhat when Osirian beliefs prevailed, for such was her popularity that she was incorporated into the new beliefs. She was often represented as the Lady of the Sycamore Tree; her cow's head half emerged from the tree, which was

growing by a river bank, and she welcomed the arrival of the deceased, pouring out water for him and proffering food. The sycamore tree perhaps belongs to the tradition that when Osiris's drowned body was washed ashore at Byblos in Phoenicia it was a sycamore tree which grew up around it and enclosed it. Hathor was also represented as a cow suckling not the living, but the dead pharaoh; she suckled other dead souls, too, either as a cow or as a woman, thus sustaining them during their mummification, their journey to the judgement hall of Osiris and the weighing of the soul. In the Late Period, while a dead man was still called an Osiris, dead women were called Hathors.

infant, who when he grew up became her guard. After the body of Osiris was recovered Anubis, who administered medicines as well as poison, provided unguents and rare medicaments with which he, or he together with Isis and Nephthys, embalmed it. Anubis then performed the funerary rites for Osiris, rites which he invented and which were the model for all burial ceremonies thereafter. According to other traditions, however, Geb was the principal officiant, assisted by Anubis and Thoth.

In later belief, Anubis had three important functions. He supervised the correct embalmment of bodies and their reconstitution. He received the mummy into the tomb, performing the Opening of the Mouth ceremony; and he then conducted the soul to the Field of Celestial Offerings, laying his hands over the mummy to protect it. Most important of all, he supervised the weighing of the soul, closely watching the scales, which were often surmounted by his head, to see if the pans balanced. His judgement was of vital importance, for it was accepted in turn by Thoth, Horus and Osiris.

Anubis was represented as a jackal-headed man; or as a dog accompanying Isis; or as a jackal or a dog couchant on a pedestal or tomb. His symbol was a black and white ox-hide spattered with blood and hanging from a pole, but the significance of this is uncertain.

Upuaut

Upuaut (or Wepwawet), a wolf-deity, was originally a local god of Asyut or Lycopolis in Middle Egypt. Having been identified with Khenti-Amentiu of Abydos, he was closely associated with Anubis and sometimes confused with him. His name meant 'Opener of the Ways', and as a war-god he seems to have been leader of the king's advance guard in war. When he became associated with Osiris, he was thought to have accompanied him on his pacific conquest, and was later called Avenger of Osiris and said to be his son. At other times, however, he seems to have been a form of Osiris and in this manifestation he was known as Sekhemtaui, 'Power of the Two Lands'.

Upuaut was said to stand at the prow of Auf-Ra's boat as it passed through the river of the Underworld, and he was also depicted in the same position in the boat of Osiris. He was chiefly revered, however, for his role as Opener of the Ways to the West, the Underworld, showing the dead souls the path through that dark realm.

Upuaut was represented as a standing wolf, or as a wolf-headed man, who was sometimes shown wearing armour and carrying weapons.

Thoth

Thoth, whose animal was an ibis or a dog-headed baboon, was an ancient deity but his origin is something of a mystery. He seems to have come from the Delta, for he had many connections with other Delta gods; but his chief cult centre was in Middle Egypt, at Eshmunen (Ashmunein) or Hermopolis. He played an important part in many myths in varying characters, but probably began as a funerary deity.

In Hermopolis, however, he sometimes replaced the 'Great Cackler' or Geb as the bird which laid the cosmic egg and thus created the world. The original Ogdoad of Hermopolis were called the 'souls of Thoth'. Thoth was created by the power of utterance, and was called the inventor of speech. He himself, according to the Hermopolitans, was self-begotten, having appeared at the dawn of time on a lotus flower.

Thoth figured equally in the Heliopolitan and Memphite cosmogonies, however, and was also described as the 'heart of Ra', that is the personification of his divine intelligence as creator as well as his tongue of creative power. He was one of the defenders manning Ra's solar barque; but his greatest service to Ra was the retrieval of his Eye when it had escaped into Nubia in the form of Tefnut. As we have remarked, it was sometimes said that Thoth married Tefnut on their return.

Ra was said to have created the moon as a reward for Thoth, or to have allowed Thoth to create it, and to have appointed Thoth as his representative in the sky by night. In other words, one of the eyes of the ancient sky-falcon became identified with Thoth, who thus assimilated a former god of the moon, Aah. He was also known as the White Disk, governor of the living star-gods; and because of his strong, measured progress across the heavens, he was called 'Bull Among the Stars'.

It was natural that the god of the moon should be associated with time, and Thoth was called Measurer of Time, which was symbolised by the notched palm-branch which he held in his hand. Again, it was easy to extend his functions from this and to call him the inventor of mathematics, astronomy and engineering. His skills as a mathematician allowed the gods to keep count of their possessions. He was thus the accountant of the gods as well as being secretary to Ra.

Mathematics and astronomy had an immediate connection for the Egyptians with magic and divination.

Thoth was a great Lord of Magic, and when he was serving as vizier to king Osiris he not only taught him the arts of civilisation, but also taught Isis the many spells which were to earn her the title of Great Enchantress. Thoth's spells enabled Isis to restore Osiris to life and to conceive by him after his murder. He also taught her the spells with which she cured all the diseases to which the young Horus fell victim while he was growing up in the Delta marshes. Thoth himself, with the authority of Ra, exorcised the deadly poison with which Set nearly killed the child. Just as Thoth retrieved Ra's Eye, so as god of medicine he was able to restore the eye of Horus when it had been torn out by Set as a black pig.

Another role of Thoth helped him in his function as great magician. This role was that of Master of the Words of God, or of the characters of writing, which he was universally said to have invented. The connection with magic is clear, for the texts were the clue to all religious mysteries. Thoth himself was supposed to have written with his own hand a book of magic and the forty-two volumes which contained all the wisdom of the world. In the Eighteenth Dynasty these volumes were brought into the courts of law for reference, for the wisdom of the divine order was largely a matter of the laws governing the Kingdom.

Thoth was known as a scribe of the gods, that is the usual recorder and imparter of their decisions and so came to be considered the messenger of the gods. For this reason he was identified with Hermes in the Greek period. But as scribe and secretary of Ra he was worshipped by scribes and all the learned men in Egypt, including of course the priests. They tended at times to inflate the role of their patron-god. For example they claimed that whereas the dead pharaoh became one with Ra during the day, during the night he was assimilated to Thoth, the moon. During the ascendancy of Amon-Ra, however, Thoth was firmly relegated to the position of scribe and god of wisdom, his function as god of the moon becoming insignificant, while that as demiurge was of course denied.

In Osirian beliefs Thoth gained new roles and added importance. As author of the sacred laws of Egypt, Thoth was seen as an upholder of justice and a mediator. This was at first his role in the great quarrel between Horus and Set. But Thoth was above all a searcher after truth; soon he had espoused the cause of righteousness and was proclaiming loud and frequently that Horus was right, Set a liar. As we have seen, Thoth acted as advocate for the family of Osiris. He defended Osiris himself so well against the tribunal of the gods called by Set that Osiris was immediately acquitted, or 'declared true of voice'. Thoth then represented the case of Horus before the tribunal. Here his task was certainly more difficult, for Horus stood before the court as an inexperienced youth who might indeed not be capable of ruling, and Set, being unsure of his ground, was clever enough to suggest that the trial be decided by physical combat. Besides, Set was supported by Ra-Harakhte, whom the gods may secretly have derided but could not thwart.

Both judge and advocate had curious experiences with Set during the course of the long dispute. For Set swallowed Ra-Harakhte's Eye, which was restored to him only after Set had been forced to vomit it up. And Thoth was born – or reborn – out of Set's head, Isis having employed her magic

to make Set pregnant, in retaliation for his sodomitic attempt on her son. Set had a great liking for lettuce, so she gathered some fresh crisp leaves and made a dish for him. He ate the dish with pleasure – and conceived. Isis had mixed the seed of Horus with the lettuce leaves. This was taken by Ra-Harakhte as a sign that Set's calumnies were untrue and helped decide the case in favour of Horus. Thereafter Thoth was most frequently associated with the Osirian hall of judgement. He stood near the scales, and as Anubis declared the result, Thoth recorded it in his ledger. Osiris accepted the word of Thoth and Anubis.

Thoth would certainly gain from the downfall of Set, as would his cult. For being like Set a god of Upper Egypt, he was able to replace him in his most important functions. Thus, together with Horus, he was seen performing the lustral ceremonies at the royal coronation, a baptism which imbued the king with the purity and strength of the Lord of the Two Lands. If Set appeared in dynastic

functions on the ancient monuments his image was often changed to that of Thoth, the similarity of his long curved snout with Thoth's ibis beak making this easy.

Thoth was most often represented as an ibis-headed man wearing the moon crescent and disk. As a god of the dead he wore attributes of Osiris: the crown with disk, *uraeus* and horns. As Aah he was represented standing on the symbol of Mayet, as a mummy, with the shaved head and sidelock of Khonsu and wearing the crescent and full moon. His silver boat transported the souls of the dead across the night sky. He was also depicted as a dog-headed baboon, the animal of an ancient god, Asten, whom he assimilated.

Seshat
Seshat, an ancient goddess who was thought to be the sister, or more usually the wife, of Thoth, was the deity of writing and of measurement before such functions were ascribed to her husband. She was called the 'Lady of Books', or celestial librarian,

Above. Thoth in his role as god of wisdom and upholder of justice has a dual role in this scene from the judgement of the dead. In his form as dog-headed baboon perched atop the scales in which the heart is weighed against Mayet (Truth and Justice), he makes sure the heart has a fair chance to justify itself; in his ibis-headed form as scribe to the gods, he uses his reed pen to record the verdict as it is delivered. To the right the deceased, the priestess Anhai, is dressed in feathers of Truth. Papyrus of Anhai. Twentieth Dynasty. British Museum, London.

Opposite above. The vulture-goddess Nekhebet hovering over the pharaoh Amenemhet III, under whose reign Egypt prospered and developed economically, peace enabling large-scale irrigation and drainage projects to be undertaken. To achieve this, the king is shown here slaying foreign enemies. The names of hostile nations occupy free spaces in the design. Pectoral from tomb of Princess Meret. Twelfth Dynasty. Egyptian Museum, Cairo.

Opposite below. Gift offerings to the goddess Sekhmet. Before her stands a priest. To the right and left are the vulture and serpent symbols of Upper and Lower Egypt, for as defender of Ra, Sekhmet was defender of the kingdom. Bronze inlaid with gold, silver and copper. c. 600 B.C. Ägyptisches Museum, East Berlin.

and was the patroness also of arithmetic, architecture and records. Though she shared these functions with Thoth, Seshat was essentially a royal deity, belonging to the pharaoh alone. Thus when temples – royal edifices – were being founded, Seshat and the pharaoh were portrayed together stretching the cord to measure out their dimensions. As recorder, she wrote down the name of the king on the leaves of the Tree of Life, near which she dwelt, thus giving him immortality; and she marked the duration of the king's earthly life on the notched palm-branch which she carried, having calculated the length of his days. In this capacity she seems to have had associations with Anubis.

Seshat was generally depicted as a woman wearing a flower or star emblem on her head, together with the *uraeus* of her royal connections. She was dressed in a leopard skin, and she usually held a pen and a scribe's ink palette.

Protective Divinities of the Pharaohs and the Kingdom

We have seen that all the local gods had in some sense a political or at least a military role, for each one was the leader of his people as a social or political group. The fortunes of the deity and those of his people rose or fell in concert. We have also seen that the god of whichever people attained pre-eminence in Egypt acquired a special significance. The leaders of that people, who were also chief priests of the deity, formed the royal house of the kingdom.

The most notable of such deities were of course Horus and Ra, both of whom were inextricably linked to the royal house through all the vicissitudes of the long Egyptian history.

Their combined strength as Ra-Harakhte impressed the solar image so firmly on the idea of a state god that all other protective divinities of the kingdom also acquired solar colouring. Such deities may have had a long history in other guises and may have possessed distinct mythologies, but inevitably when they grew to national importance they were identified with the sun cults of the pharaohs. This was true even at times in early and later Egyptian history when Osiris was the most enthusiastically and popularly worshipped of the gods. Even though Osirian mythology had been somewhat adapted to the state religion, Osiris could not compete in this world with the sun cults which were the moral basis of government, of the divine order, or of the equilibrium held by the pharaoh between dual poles – a characteristic of Egyptian thought.

This duality was stressed in the distinction always made between Upper and Lower Egypt – even at times when unification of the Two Lands was unquestioned: the strength of the pharaoh was to be measured by his success in uniting the two. Though Nekhebet and Buto, the protective goddesses of the two kingdoms, were united in the royal insignia, they never ceased to be considered separately.

Nekhebet

Nekhebet was a vulture-goddess of Upper Egypt whose city was Nekheb, on the opposite bank of the Nile from Nekhen or Hierakonpolis, a cult centre of the falcon-god Horus. The two cities were associated in prehistoric times as capital of Upper Egypt. The importance of Nekhebet rose with that of Horus, unifier of the Two Lands, but whereas he became firmly linked with Lower Egypt too, Nekhebet remained attached only to the South, as its protective deity. The chief god of her kingdom was Set in early times; but after his disgrace and replacement by Thoth, Nekhebet gained fresh importance. Where before Horus and Set performed the symbolic gestures of *samtaui*, increasingly Nekhebet and Buto symbolised

the union of the Two Lands.

Nekhebet was absorbed into the solar mythology, being called the daughter of Ra and his right eye. She was also drawn into the Osirian sphere as wife of Khenti-Amentiu, First of the Westerners; the idea was no doubt suggested by the fact that the humble dead were thrown to the desert where their bodies became carrion for vultures. Nekhebet was equally associated with the fertility aspects of Osirianism, being considered the wife of Hapi, the Nile, who opened the gates to allow the Nile to flow from the primeval ocean. Hence she was thought of as a mother-goddess, protectress of childbirth and, as the 'great wild cow', identified with Hathor.

Usually Nekhebet was represented as a woman, or as a vulture wearing the white crown of Upper Egypt, when she was known as the Lady of Dread. She was protective especially of the king, and was depicted spreading her wings above him and in this position holding in her talons the royal ring or whisk.

Buto

Buto, more correctly known as Udjat or Edjo, was a cobra-goddess whose original home and chief cult centre was in the Delta marshes. As Nekhebet was the motherly protectress of the pharaoh, so Buto was his aggressive defender. She was seen as the *uraeus* cobra worn on the brow first of Ra and then of all the pharaohs, her hood spread in a menacing attitude, ready to spit poison on the pharaoh's enemies or to burn them

up with her fiery glance. It is sometimes thought that in early times her power could be turned against the pharaoh himself, her bite being the death instrument administered by Anubis at the appointed time for the pharaoh's death.

As we have seen, the *uraeus* was the left eye of Ra which, after it asserted its own independence, the sun-god placed in a position of honour on his brow. Buto thus personified the sun's burning heat and was known as Lady of Heaven and queen of all the gods. She was closely associated with Horus the Elder in his rise to supremacy in Lower Egypt; and she was associated with Horus the Younger, having befriended Isis and become the child's foster-mother. Other ways were also found to bring her into the Osirian system: she was called the daughter of Anubis and named 'the Green One' or 'she who supplies cool water', thus paralleling the association of Nekhebet with the Nile. From the goddess's temple at Buto the 'Great Green', or Mediterranean, could be seen.

Buto was represented as a woman wearing the *uraeus*, or the red crown of Lower Egypt. This crown, known as the Lady of Spells, gave her another link with the Great Enchantress, Isis: there was a famous oracle in her temple at Buto. She was represented carrying a papyrus stem round which was coiled a cobra, and sometimes shown simply as a cobra coiled in a basket supported by papyrus plants and wearing the crown of Lower Egypt. At other times the crown itself stood for Buto – generally as a constituent of the double crown or *pschent*, which was called the Lady of Power or the Lady of Flame, and which symbolised the supreme power of the pharaoh over the Two Lands.

Harsaphes

Harsaphes (or Herishef), a local god of Heracleopolis Magna in the Faiyum, became a national deity during the First Intermediate Period, when his followers overcame the Asiatic invaders in the Delta and united Middle and Lower Egypt under their rule.

Left. A limestone figure inscribed with the name of a devotee of Mont. British Museum, London.

Right. Mont of Hermonthis, near Thebes, represented as a human-headed warrior, the war-god of the pharaoh. He was known as the defender and living soul of Ra-Harakhte, and for a time during the Eleventh Dynasty became the chief protective deity of the kingdom.

Opposite. The god Amon in the form of a ram wearing a triple crown. Above him rises the goddess Edjo or Buto as a winged *uraeus* with the sundisk on her head, ready to protect Amon as she protects the pharaoh. Before Amon sits the spirit of world order, Mayet.

Their rule over Upper Egypt was only nominal and they were eventually supplanted by the Thebans and Mont. Harsaphes was a ram-deity, represented by a ram-headed man. He was a god of fertility and connected with water, his name meaning 'He who is on his lake'. As a national deity he was considered to be a form of Horus.

Mont

Mont (or Montu) was the local god of Hermonthis, a city about ten miles south of Thebes, and capital of the Theban nome. He rose to national prominence in the Eleventh Dynasty, when the pharaohs came from Hermonthis. The inevitable royal connection with Ra led to the solarisation of Mont, and Hermonthis became a great centre of the sun cult, known as the Heliopolis of the South.

Mont was known as a form of Ra-Harakhte and was called the 'living soul of Ra'. As his ancient sacred animal was the bull, he was called the 'Bull of the mountains of Sunrise and Sunset'. However, he also personified the destructive force of the sun, and was called the 'Bull of the Mighty Arm'. In the New Kingdom his function became specialised as the war-god of the pharaoh. He was depicted leading defeated enemies to the pharaoh and handing him the *khepesh*, his sickle-shaped sword.

Mont was represented as a bull-headed man carrying bow and arrows, a club and a knife. In late times he was said to be incarnate in the bull Buchis. In his solar aspect, Mont was shown as a falcon-headed man wearing on his head the solar disk and *uraeus* between two tall plumes. He was thought to stand on the prow of the night-barque of the sun, slaying the sun's enemies with his lance. In this position as a defender of the pharaoh and the sun, Mont became firmly established as a dynastic figure rather than as a popular deity.

Sebek

Sebek (or Suchos or Sobk) was a crocodile-deity, the ancient city god of Crocodilopolis in the Faiyum, an area of lake and marshland in Lower Egypt. He was a water-god, whose name meant 'He who causes to be pregnant or fertile', and was said to be the son of Neith of Sais.

At first he was a relatively humble deity who at the command of Ra performed tasks such as catching with his net the four sons of Horus as they emerged from the waters in a lotus bloom. Sebek rose to become the god of the pharaohs in the Twelfth Dynasty – after the first rise of Amon, but before his real ascendancy in the Eighteenth Dynasty. During that period the pharaohs moved their capital to the entrance of the Faiyum, which they brought under cultivation through the construction of irrigation and drainage schemes. The principal cult centre of Sebek remained the Faiyum, but after the Twelfth Dynasty he was worshipped everywhere and

acquired another important sanctuary in Upper Egypt at Ombos (Kom Ombo). This later encouraged his identification with Set: when Set was in disgrace he had the form of a crocodile. Sebek was also worshipped at Thebes and at Lake Moeris.

In Middle Kingdom *Coffin Texts* Sebek was sometimes identified with Maka, a fifty-foot flint-armoured and knife-slashing serpent which confronted the solar barque as it entered the Underworld; he was thus a personification of evil. But in most parts of Egypt his fierce aspect was admired. His period as state god allowed his identification with the sun, as Sebek-Ra. We have seen how the *aart* that cured Geb was transformed into Sebek. A variant of this myth relates that when Ra-Harmakhis was fighting his enemies by the sacred lake near Het Nebes the struggle went against him until he took refuge in the lake. There he was transformed into a falcon-headed crocodile, and was able to vanquish his enemies. (In fact the god of the nome in which Sebek's cult centre was established was a falcon-deity.) Thereafter Sebek was a royal, solar god, often identified with the divine king

Geb. In Osirian belief he was said to have been the form which Horus took in order to retrieve the parts of Osiris's body cast into the Nile by Set. He remained a fearsome though generally beneficent deity far into the Late Period, when a sacred crocodile was kept at Lake Moeris, decorated with precious stones and gold.

Sebek was represented as a mummified crocodile or as a man with a crocodile-head wearing horns like those of Amon-Ra, the solar disk, and two *uraeus* serpents each wearing a solar disk.

Amon

During the whole of the Old Kingdom Amon was an obscure god of the city of Thebes – of less importance even than Mont, god of the neighbouring city of Hermonthis, capital of the Theban nome. Little is known of his original character – and indeed little was known even by the ancient Egyptians, who called him by a name meaning 'the hidden'.

More than any other deity, Amon was the creation of political circumstances, gradually acquiring new characteristics as he assimilated the mythological roles of other gods after

the defeat of their followers. More than any other god, Amon and the power ascribed to him bolstered the authority of his early followers when they became the royal house.

The princes of Thebes and Mont together with Amon came to prominence about 2050 B.C., at the end of the First Intermediate Period, when they reunited Egypt under their rule. During the Middle Kingdom Amon was considered chiefly as a creative god. He was represented as a goose and called, like Geb, the Great Cackler, who laid the cosmic egg. It seems that the identification with the Great Cackler was based on the virile reputation of the bird; but it was not pursued and, with the exception of the pinion feathers which remained an attribute of Amon, the goose image was dropped.

More important was the association in the Middle Kingdom with another fertile animal, the ram. Amon was said once to have disguised himself in the head and skin of a ram which he had flayed and beheaded when Shu, god of the atmosphere, begged him to come out of hiding. After Amon had shown himself to the world in this guise rams were sacred to him, inviolate except once a year, when a ram was flayed and beheaded in offering to him. As we have seen, in the cosmogonies Amon usurped Shu's life-giving functions and himself became a god of the wind which stirred up Nun and thus began creation. The soul of Amon was said to be enshrined either in a ram-sphinx or in a serpent-sceptre called Kamatef. Amon was also represented as an ithyphallic man with blue-black skin, wearing tall plumes, and sometimes as a mummy, like the other creator-gods, Ptah and Min. Amon borrowed many of the characteristics of Min. Later he also became identified with Mont as 'Bull of his Mother' and as a war-god, for the Theban princes were the strongest nucleus of resistance to foreign influence. As their power grew, so Amon gradually became solarised and was henceforth known as Amon-Ra. He wore all the symbols of supreme power of the sun-god, his head sometimes being shown as a *uraeus*. He entered the realms of the dead too, when his ram-head allowed easy identification with the dead form of that god, Auf-Ra, sailing through the Underworld and giving renewed life to the souls of the dead.

The period of greatest glory for Amon-Ra followed the expulsion of the foreign Hyksos pharaohs by the princes of Thebes and the second reunification of the Two Lands under their rule in about 1570 B.C. Egypt had in some ways benefited from the rule of Hyksos kings, for they had introduced the techniques of the Bronze Age. The Thebans had learnt from them new arts of war and agriculture. At the opening of the New Kingdom Egypt was not only strengthened by reunification, but before long was enriched by Asian conquests, whose tribute poured into the coffers of the Theban god.

New temples to Amon-Ra were built everywhere, and especially at and around Thebes. One of the most famous was the temple of Amenhotep III at Luxor, dedicated to the ithyphallic Amon-Ra. This was not far from the greatest temple of Amon, at Karnak, where he was regarded more

as a god of the wind. Nearby, on the western bank of the Nile, were the royal mortuary temples, lying below the crags of western Thebes where, from Amenhotep I onwards, the pharaohs were buried in the rock-hewn tombs of the Valley of the Kings – thus abandoning the Osirian Abydos as a royal burial ground.

During the New Kingdom Amon-Ra became known as the 'king of the gods'. Dominion over a great empire stretching from the Euphrates through to the Sudan led to the conception of Amon-Ra as greatest of all the gods, the universal 'Lord of the Thrones of the World'. But Amon-Ra was not simply god of victory and ruler of the other deities: he also embodied their several functions and characteristics. He was said to be able to take any form he wished, each of the gods being one of his forms. He did this so that his names might be many; but his real name was secret, as was Ra's, so that the other gods could not pray to him. He emerged out of the primeval flood on to the mound of Hermopolis, where he hatched, self-created, from an egg. The goddess of heaven, Amaunet (his own name feminised, though in fact she was a more ancient deity than Amon), received him there in the form of a cow. Mounting on her back, Amon swam about the waters of Nun, and wherever he landed he became the local god. He was especially associated with the gods of creation and fertility: the ram-gods Harsaphes of Heracleopolis and Banebdetet of Mendes, Nun, Hapi the Nile, Ptah of Memphis, Min of Koptos and Mont of Thebes. Amon was thus the universal creator: he became head of the Theban Ennead and of the Hermopolitan Ogdoad, usurping Thoth, and was identified with Ra-Atum of Heliopolis as creator. He was often called the face of Ra and the body of Ptah.

Like earlier forms of the sun-god, Amon-Ra was held to be the physical father of the pharaoh, for heirs to the throne were said to be conceived by his union with the queen in the form of the reigning pharaoh; in fact the pharaoh wore the insignia of Amon-

Above. The crocodile-god Sebek, wearing the horns of Amon-Ra. Sebek became a royal god when the Twelfth-Dynasty pharaohs established their capital in his Lower Egyptian homeland, the Faiyum, which they developed greatly. Not content with such realistic representations as this Ptolemaic bronze figure, Late Period worshippers kept a live bejewelled crocodile at Lake Moeris. British Museum, London.

Opposite. Ram-headed deity from the tomb of Thuthmosis III. In the period leading up to and during the Eighteenth Dynasty myths were elaborated to enable the Theban Amon-Ra to absorb the traditions of several ram-deities, notably one in which he disguised himself in the skin of a flayed and beheaded ram, which also explained his usurpation of Shu's role. 1450 B.C. British Museum, London.

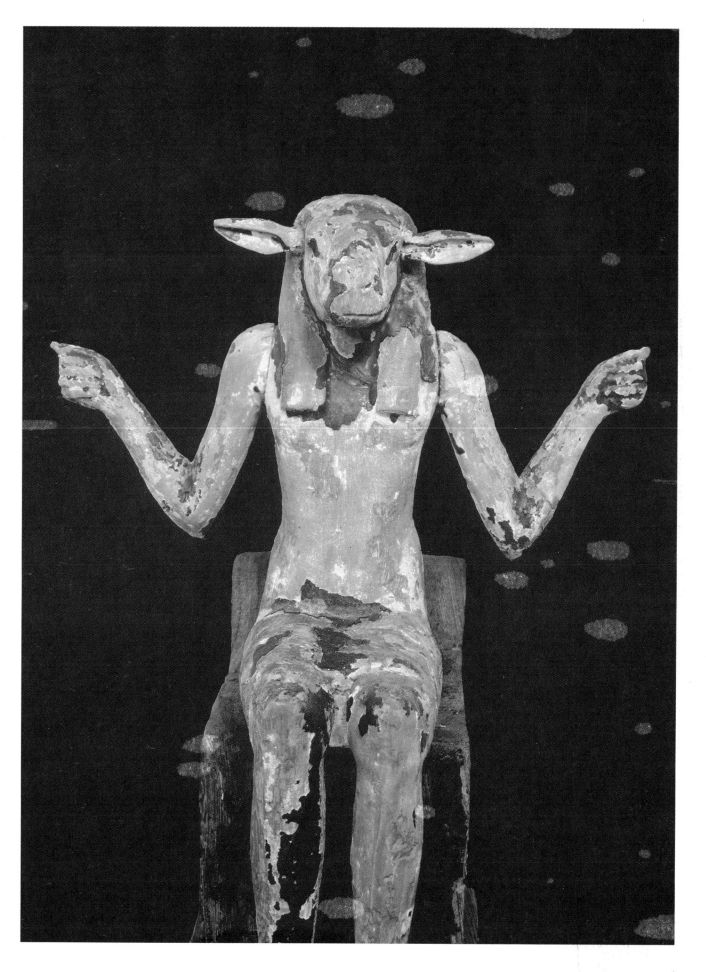

Ra when, with great publicity, he approached the queen. Amon-Ra's 'sons' of course built temples in honour of their father, and he in turn led them to military victory, infusing them with the breath of life and giving them the strength of a hundred thousand men. This belief accounted for Alexander's peaceful conquest of Egypt, for when he arrived there he went through a ceremony at the oasis of Amon-Ra which gave him rebirth as the son of the great god and entitled him to wear the curved ram's horns of Amon.

In addition Amon-Ra had cosmic functions, for having created all things he ordered time and the seasons, sailed over the heavens and the Underworld in his solar barque, controlled the winds and clouds – giving orders in his voice of thunder – and sustained all creatures and vegetation.

Despite his universal grandeur, his cosmic and dynastic associations, Amon-Ra was also a popular god, whose worship among humble people was universal and personal. He was called the vizier of the poor, incorruptible and anxious to see that the just attained their rightful deserts and that the weak were protected against the strong. As a loving father, Amon-Ra was a compassionate god; but he was not to be thwarted by magic rites, for he was known as a breaker of spells – his suppliants had to justify their requests by demonstrating their good character or confessing to their sins.

This sort of personal worship of the state god broke with earlier Egyptian traditions. An even greater break with tradition arose from the role of the priesthood of Amon. Though theologically Amon-Ra was identified with earlier forms of the sun-god as the dynastic deity, in fact his unprecedented wealth and power led to a novel form of theocracy. Where the strength of the god would before have bolstered the royal house, in the case of Amon-Ra it eventually undermined the monarchy. Part of this movement can be ascribed to the resentment of the priests of Ra at Heliopolis, who maintained their independence and cherished their own deity as the only

Right. The head of Queen Akmet, mother of Hatshepsut. Hatshepsut was at pains to emphasise her divine descent; this is one of the reliefs from Hatshepsut's mortuary temple at Deir el Bahri which show how Akmet conceived and bore her after union with Amon. Eighteenth Dynasty.

Opposite. Akhenaten (the heretical Amenhotep IV) and his wife Nefertiti worshipping the sun-disk Aten, whose rays bear hands with which to receive offerings and offer the *ankh*, sign of life. Akhenaten himself offers the *ankh* to his god, whom he claimed to equal in divinity. Eighteenth Dynasty. Egyptian Museum, Cairo.

'true' sun-god. But the priests of Amon-Ra themselves sowed the seeds of their downfall. Increasingly their wealth brought them secular power and the desire to interfere in 'political' life. As we have seen, in the Eighteenth Dynasty, Hatshepsut owed her position on the throne to the support of the Amon-Ra priesthood; consequently she was passionately devoted to Amon-Ra, building her temple at Deir el-Bahri in his honour. The priesthood was closely linked to the royal house, but therefore subject to ambition and dissensions. Its exclusiveness together with its instability reflected on the royal authority and weakened it.

This situation set the stage for a reaction, and a return to archaic worship of the sun in its 'pure' form of the Aten, the sun-disk. The movement received further impetus from imperial expansion into Asia which brought knowledge of Near Eastern deities and monotheism. It was a short-lived but profoundly disruptive interlude, begun by Thuthmosis IV and Amenhotep III and brought to a

fanatical climax by Amenhotep IV, who changed his name (which meant 'Amon is content') to Akhenaten (which meant 'It pleases Aten'). Akhenaten dispossessed Amon-Ra's priesthood, despoiled his temples and abandoned Thebes as the capital city. But already before his death he was seeking to come to a compromise, for the neglected empire was disintegrating, and his successors Tutankhamon and especially Horemheb devoted great labours to restoring the temples and making reparations to the god.

If the Akhenaten interlude had taught his successors anything, however, it was that the royal house should not be overly dependent on one universal deity. Horemheb took care to embellish the temples of the other gods as well, and Thebes was never again the political capital of Egypt. The Amon-Ra priesthood explained this by a legend that the city could not be ruled by an earthly prince, for it belonged to the divine Amon. Once more the ambition revealed by this explanation led to their downfall. They sought a link with the

Above. Amon-Ra receiving offerings from Seti I. Nineteenth Dynasty. British Museum, London.

Opposite above. Head of Khons, the moon-god and son of Amon and Mut in the Theban Triad. He is depicted with the shaven head of youth. He had special associations with the birth of kings and with fertility. Granite. Late Eighteenth Dynasty.

Opposite below. Khons Hor, an amalgamation of Horus son of Ra, the 'living Horus' or pharaoh, and Khons, son of Amon, whose son the pharaohs were said to be from the Eighteenth Dynasty onwards. Khons Hor was a form particularly worshipped at Ombos (Kom Ombo), Set's ancient cult centre, for Khons was sometimes said to have helped Horus overcome Set. Twenty-second Dynasty, c. 850 B.C.

ruling house by making a royal princess the Divine Consort of Amon-Ra. She was his high priestess and the representative of his government on earth. Such a doctrine made it important for each pharaoh to gain acceptance for his own daughter as 'spiritual daughter' of the high priestess.

The doctrine was an attempt by the priests not only to regain secular power, but to restore their position at the head of a co-ordinated, nationwide priesthood of all the gods. Yet the Theban priesthood ruled like any other secular power and set themselves up in semi-rivalry to the pharaohs ruling in the north. The rivalry was not altogether eliminated by the appointment of members of the royal house to the high priesthood; for they tended to treat it as a titular appointment only and did not take up residence at Thebes. The priesthood made much of the oracle of Amon-Ra, whose utterances were used to secure their political ends. The ultimate result of all this was that when Thebes was conquered by the Assyrians in 663 B.C. Amon-Ra fell with the kingdom. All forms of sun-worship were dropped in favour of Osirianism.

Aten

Aten was a form of the sun-god from the earliest times, representing the sun at its zenith, open and strong. It was depicted as a red disk with rays stretching down to earth. In the religion evolved by Akhenaten it was divorced from the other aspects of the sun and indeed from all other gods and theological systems, being considered the supreme power of life and a combination of Ra-Harakhte and Shu. By the openness with which it revealed itself to mankind, the Aten contrasted with Amon-Ra; but in the claim that all men – Egyptian and foreign – were the children of Aten, the new cult resembled the universal appeal of Amon-Ra – and Atenism surpassed the cult of Amon-Ra through claiming that its god was not just the supreme deity and fount of all the others, but was in fact the only god worthy of worship. Nevertheless

in his famous hymn Akhenaten claimed to be the sole intermediary of the god, and equal in divinity to Aten. Atenism also seems to have reverted to the old idea of immortality for the pharaoh alone. The material life of this world was the only one that existed for ordinary people.

It has been said that one of the motives of Akhenaten in promoting his new religion was to find a god which could be worshipped as an abstract yet ever-present being – without specifically Egyptian associations – by all the peoples of his empire. As we have repeatedly observed, however, the Egyptians themselves were not given to exclusive cults: they preferred a syncretistic faith built on old traditions. Such an abstract yet materialistic faith could not survive and began to crumble even before the death of its founder. The movement, supported only by parvenu courtiers, had upset the old power structure. Akhenaten called himself the 'King who lives in Truth', but his later detractors were able to say that during his reign Mayet was overthrown in the kingdom. The common people may have obediently abandoned Amon-Ra, but it was to turn to the old popular deities such as Bes and Taueret.

There was no time during Akhenaten's seventeen-year reign for a mythology to grow up around Aten – nor perhaps could one have developed, owing to the nature of the deity. But the wealth seized from Amon-Ra was put to good use in the construction of temples and palaces at the new northern capital of Akhetaten ('Horizon of the Aten'), now Tell el-Amarna. Here the bas-reliefs repeatedly depicted Akhenaten, his queen Nefertiti, their daughters and the pharaoh's parents Amenhotep III and Queen Tiy doing homage to the Aten; the rays emanating from the great sun-disk ended in human hands which held the symbol of life, gathered up the offerings from the altar and bestowed material blessings on mankind. Under Tutankhamon and Horemheb the names of the Aten and Akhetaten were as vigorously expunged from monuments as those of

was originally a vulture-goddess of Thebes, and was confused with Nekhebet as protectress of Upper Egypt. In the Eighteenth Dynasty, after Amon had risen to prominence, she was married to him and identified with his earlier wife Amaunet. The marriage of Mut and Amon was one of the great annual celebrations during the New Kingdom. Amon would be borne from his temple at Karnak and a great procession would embark on the Nile to visit Mut at her temple at Luxor. This ceremony was the occasion for oracular pronouncements by Amon.

Despite being considered the consort of Amon, Mut was said to be bisexual, a way of reinforcing her position as mother of all living things. She was identified with other important goddesses and called Great Sorceress, Mistress of Heaven and Eye of Ra, besides being queen of all the gods. She was generally represented as a woman, sometimes with the whole body of a vulture forming her head, wearing the *uraeus* and the double crown of Upper and Lower Egypt, which she borrowed from the pharaohs who came from her city.

Bast

Bast (or Bastet) was a local deity of the Delta, who appears as early as the Second Dynasty. Her early fetish was the cat – the wild variety domesticated, which was admired for its virility, strength and agility. Though she remained a local deity, Bast was soon connected with Ra, whose daughter and wife she was said to be, and with the Osirian deities. Bast herself was said to defend Ra against the serpent Apep. Maahes, her son by Ra, depicted as a man with a lion-head wearing the *atef* crown of Osiris, or as a lion devouring a captive, was sometimes identified with Horus of Praises, a form of Horus the Younger. At other times Maahes was identified with Nefertum the son of Sekhmet, with whom her priests tried to fuse Bast. This identification was attempted in the Twenty-second Dynasty when, beginning with Sheshonq I, the pharaohs, who were of Libyan origin, made their capital near Bast's

Amon-Ra and the other gods had been under the heretic pharaoh; but some examples of the realistic art of the period have survived, including those at the other Aten temples at Thebes and Heliopolis, where Aten was equated with Ra.

Khons

Khons (or Khonsu) came to prominence relatively late as a moon-god of Thebes. As Amon was one of the Hermopolitan Ogdoad and already associated with the moon-god Thoth, it was natural that for the 'son' of his triad at Thebes he should choose the neighbouring moon-god Khons. Accordingly Amon and Mut were said to be the parents of Khons. It seems that Khons originally represented the placenta of the king. The king being of divine origin, all that pertained to his birth was divine; and as the king was identified with the sun, so the afterbirth was identified with the moon. A mummified placenta was borne on a standard as part

of the regalia on state occasions.

As the moon, Khons was described as a runner who scoured the skies, his name being interpreted to mean 'to traverse'. At Thebes he was identified with Thoth as reckoner of time and with Shu as god of the heavens or atmosphere. Called the Lord of Truth and maker of destinies, Khons was a giver of oracles. He was also revered as a spell breaker for his authority over evil spirits. Finally, like his parents, he was a source of fertility and growth, giver of the breath of life. Khons was represented as a mummified young man, shaven except for the sidelock of youth and wearing the *menat*, symbol of virility, and the lunar disk and crescent. Sometimes he was identified with Horus and depicted falcon-headed.

Mut

Mut, Lady of Asheru in Thebes, was considered to be the great and mighty divine mother. In predynastic times her name meant simply 'vulture'; she city of Bubastis and adopted the goddess as their own. The temples at Bubastis were enriched, and a great new shrine was built at Thebes.

As state deity in the Late Period, Bast was regarded as a kindly goddess representing the beneficent powers of the sun protecting the Two Lands, and was sometimes said to personify the moon; Sekhmet, on the other hand, represented the destructive powers of the sun and popular belief distinguished her clearly from Bast. Bast also acquired some of the characteristics of Hathor, being known as the goddess of joy, music and dancing. Her cult was celebrated in light-hearted barge processions and in orgiastic ceremonies. She was depicted as a woman with a cat's head, carrying a sistrum, a box or basket and the head of a lioness surrounded by many concentric necklaces. Cats were treated as sacred in honour of Bast and the great cemetery of mummified cats at Bubastis was famous in the ancient world.

Neith

Neith was an ancient goddess of hunting whose worship at Sais in the western Delta dated from predynastic times. Her cult sign, a shield and crossed arrows, suggests that she may have been a warlike goddess. It is thought that she may have been the deity of an early confederation of Lower Egypt, for she wore the red crown of Lower Egypt. From early times she acquired the titles Great Goddess and mother of the gods, for though often called the daughter of Ra she was said to have borne Ra before her own creation out of Nun, and was at times thought of as the personification of the waters of chaos. In later times she was said to be the mother of Sebek, Isis, Horus and Osiris, who, it was claimed, was buried at Sais. Still later, at the time of her greatest power in the Saite Period, the pharaoh Nectanebo II claimed her as his mother. In short, Neith was regarded as the universal mother and guardian of men and gods. As a creative deity she was said to be the wife of Khnum at Elephantine.

Neith also looked after the dead,

standing with Nephthys at the head of coffins and acting as one of the four goddesses guarding the Canopic jars. As 'Opener of the Ways', she was a female Anubis. In the Eighteenth Dynasty she was identified with Hathor as protectress of women. In the Saite Period, when trade in wool was important, she became a patroness of the domestic arts, her arrow attribute being taken as a weaver's shuttle. A further association was made with the knot of Isis, and powers as a sorceress were ascribed to Neith. She was appealed to for her wisdom as an arbitrator during the great quarrel of Horus and Set.

Neith rose to her greatest glory as state deity during the century and a half of the Saite Period, or the Twenty-sixth Dynasty, when kings coming from Sais reunited Lower, Middle, and then Upper Egypt after the invasion by the Assyrians. During this period the tendency was to archaism in art and religion and a search for past glories suited to the worship of an ancient goddess. Great new temples were built at Sais, and the monolithic shrines with obelisks and sacred lakes were closely described by Herodotus, as well as the tombs of the kings, who were now buried at Sais.

Neith was depicted as a woman wearing the red crown of Lower Egypt, in which she was said to be immanent, and bearing a bow and crossed arrows. Occasionally she was represented as the great cow mother who bore Ra daily.

Divinities of Creation, Fertility and Birth

Ptah

Ptah, one of the most potent of the Egyptian creator-gods, originated in late predynastic times as a local god of Memphis, though his cult was supposedly instituted by Menes, the first pharaoh. It is said that his antiquity is proved by the fact that he was represented with legs together and arms close to his body – showing that his representation was fixed at an early time when sculptors were technically

Above. Ptah, according to Memphite teaching architect of the universe and god of creation, was known as the divine artificer and the patron of the fine arts. His secondary role as funerary deity was increasingly emphasised, no doubt under the influence of this traditional representation as a mummified figure. Nineteenth Dynasty. British Museum, London.

Opposite. Horus Behdety, the winged sun-disk, hovering over a scene of ritual communion between pharaoh and god. A position of honour in shrines was assigned to Horus by Ra after his successful military campaign against Set at Edfu and re-establishment of a unified kingdom. Beneath, Thuthmosis III (Eighteenth Dynasty) honours the newly powerful deity Amon-Ra by pouring a libation and offering fire. From Hathor chapel of Thuthmosis III at Deir el-Bahri, now in Egyptian Museum, Cairo.

unable to produce separate limbs. In later times this form was said to be that of a mummy and Ptah became a god of the dead. But like other funerary deities, notably Osiris, Ptah was primarily a god of fertility.

The cosmogony of Memphis made Ptah the very fount of all creation, the oldest being imaginable. In the course of time he was identified with all the other creator-gods, and in the Nineteenth Dynasty was associated with Ra and Amon in the government of the universe and was seen as the father of the pharaoh. He was said to have taken the form of the Ram of Mendes in order to father Rameses II and to fashion him as Lord of the Two Lands, a title given to pharaohs but also applied to Ptah as founder of the political order in Egypt. As the

lord of creation, Ptah was considered to be a great magician and lord of serpents and fish. He was unusual among creator-gods in that his means of creation were spiritual rather than physical – and this certainly contributed to the fact that though he retained his importance throughout the dynastic period, Ptah never appealed strongly to popular imagination.

The philosophical nature of Ptah's creation was the product of theological speculation. To ordinary people, however, Ptah retained what was probably his oldest character as 'Greatest of Craftsmen', a natural role for the god of a great trading centre where many crafts, including metalwork and shipbuilding, were carried on. Ptah was the Divine Artificer, a skilled engineer, stonemason and metalworker. He was also patron of the fine arts, and artists were apt to call themselves High Priest of Ptah.

Ptah was associated with many other deities, including Nun, the waters of chaos from which the universe emerged; Hapi, the Nile god and source of fertility; Geb, the earth, and Tenen, an ancient earth-god personifying the primeval mound; Shu, 'lifter up of heaven'; and even the Aten. In later times Ptah was especially identified with the funerary gods Osiris and, later, Seker.

Memphis was, of course, traditionally the most ancient dynastic city, in which the pharaohs celebrated their coronations and their jubilee *sed*-festivals. Thus Ptah came naturally to be associated with the divine order and basis of their power, Mayet. He was often represented standing on the measuring reed of a workman, also interpreted as the pedestal of Mayet, as Lord of Truth or Justice, overseer of artisans, who would not overlook the deeds of any man. In his character as judge, Ptah fitted equally into his creative and Osirian roles.

Ptah was represented most frequently as a mummified man with shaven head, side whiskers and Puntite beard. From the back of his neck hung the *menat* of virility, and his two hands emerged from the mummy wrappings to grasp a sceptre tipped with the symbol of stability and, often, a *djed* symbol. By the Middle Kingdom the *djed*-column of Osiris, which seems to have been a symbol of vegetation and fertility, was deified and transferred as an attribute to Ptah. Sometimes Ptah was not mummified, but was represented as a living man wearing horns, solar disk and plumes, thus resembling certain forms of Osiris. In the Twenty-sixth Dynasty Ptah was worshipped in the form of the Apis bull.

The Memphite triad consisted of Ptah, Sekhmet and their son Nefertum. Other offspring of Ptah were the 'patakoi', deformed children who were friendly to men, and Imhotep, the renowned vizier who was the great architect of the Step Pyramid at Saqqara and was later deified.

Sekhmet

Sekhmet, consort of Ptah and goddess of the Memphite triad, was brought into conjunction with the creator-god because of the geographical proximity of her cult rather than because she shared her husband's functions. Her role was that as defender of the divine order, not as creator of it; and mythology associated her more with her father Ra than with her husband Ptah.

Sekhmet's title was the 'Mighty One' and she was a fierce goddess of war and strife and bringer of destruction to the enemies of Ra. In fact she was considered the Eye of Ra, representing the scorching, destructive power of the sun. As we have seen, Hathor took the form of Sekhmet in the legend of the Destruction of Mankind, her fury becoming so uncontrollable that she would have annihilated the human race if Ra had not had pity and made her drunk. In commemoration of this near escape, orgiastic drinking festivals were held in honour of her. Sekhmet was placed as the *uraeus* serpent on Ra's brow, where she guarded the sun-god's head and spat forth flames at his enemies.

As we have remarked, Sekhmet was sometimes identified with Bast; and occasionally she was associated with Mut: as many as six hundred statues of Sekhmet adorned the entrance to the temple of Mut.

Sekhmet was usually represented as a woman with the head of a lioness wearing the solar disk and the *uraeus*; but she was also depicted with a head formed of a crocodile or of the Eye of Ra, the *udjat*. Sometimes Sekhmet was shown like Min, with her upraised arm brandishing a knife.

Nefertum

Nefertum, an ancient god in Lower Egypt, was adopted early as the son of Ptah and Sekhmet in the Memphite triad. His name meant 'lotus' and as a lotus he was assigned an important role in creation myths. Nefertum was called Atum or Ra the Younger, for he was the boy who rose from the lotus flower in the Sea of Sacred Knives of the Hermopolitan cosmogony, and from whose tears sprang mankind. His life-giving aspect was associated with his role as god of the lotus and so the source of precious unguents.

Nefertum was represented as a lion-headed man wearing a headdress composed of a lotus flower, two plumes and two *menats*, symbols of virility or pleasure. He was called the 'Watcher at the Nostrils of Ra', thus sharing his mother's protective functions, and Ra was often depicted holding a lotus flower to his nose.

Khnum

Khnum, whose name meant 'to create' and who was called Lord of the Cool Water, was an ancient god of the First Cataract of the Nile in Upper Egypt. Here, on the island of Elephantine, the Nile was said to emerge from the Underworld or the subterranean ocean of Nun through two caverns. Khnum thus controlled the principal element of fertility in Egypt, sending half the water to the south and half to the north.

His chief cult centres were the islands of Philae and Elephantine. That at Elephantine was specially well endowed, for in the Third Dynasty, after a seven-year drought, Imhotep persuaded King Djoser to present Khnum with twelve tracts of land on either side of the Nile at Elephantine, so that Khnum would allow the Nile through. Another major temple of Khnum was at Esna, on the west bank of the Nile between Thebes and Edfu.

Khnum was self-created and was the maker of heaven, raising it on its fours pillars. He was also the maker of earth, of the Underworld and of water, of things which are and of things which shall be. He was the creator of the gods and of men, which he fashioned from clay on a potter's wheel. On the orders of Amon-Ra, Khnum fashioned the body and *ka* or soul of Hatshepsut, which was implanted in her mother by Amon-Ra after Khnum had endowed it with its surpassing beauty. In fact Khnum was said to fashion the body of every child born. He, Amon and Ptah were sometimes called the Lords of Destiny. Occasionally Khnum was called Lord of the Afterlife.

Khnum was represented as a man wearing the head of a ram with horizontal wavy horns (an animal which became extinct in the Middle Kingdom), or as a ram standing on its hind legs, which was called the 'living soul of Ra'. Sometimes he was represented with four ram's heads — an allusion to his four principal cult centres. He was said to personify the creative powers of the sun-god Ra in parts of Egypt where he was not recognised as the supreme creator-god; for his cult, being connected with the Nile, spread widely. He was also sometimes associated with Horus the Elder and depicted with a falcon-head. As a water-god he was shown holding out his hands to let water flow over them.

Heket

Heket was a water-goddess in the form of a frog or a frog-headed

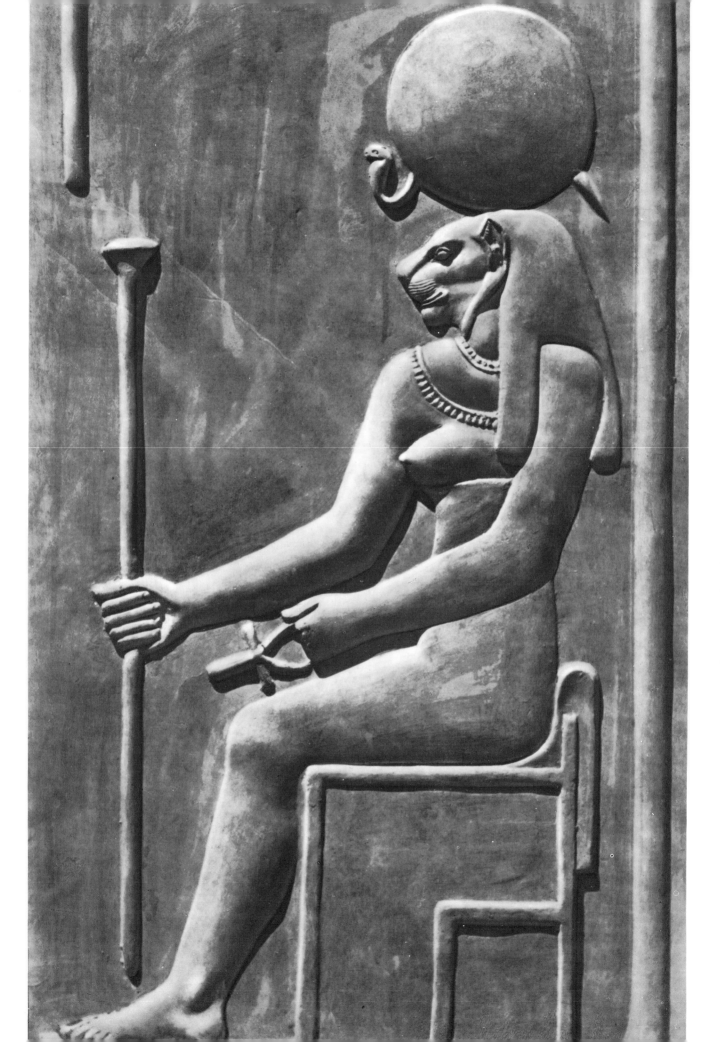

woman. At Hermopolis she was linked with the four frog-deities who lived in Nun before creation, and at Abydos was thought to have been born of Ra simultaneously with Shu and to have been his wife. As symbol of fecundity and resurrection, Heket, who helped Osiris to rise from the dead, presided over the births of kings and queens. She was usually called the wife of Khnum and became a birth-deity of all his creatures. She gave life to the bodies of the rulers, such as Hatshepsut, and to those of the men and women whom Khnum fashioned on his potter's wheel. Sometimes Heket was taken for a form of Hathor and called the mother of Horus the Elder.

Satis

Satis (also called Sati or Satet) was a goddess of fertility and love whose cult centre was on the island of Siheil, near the First Cataract. Her name meant 'to sow seed'. Before long she usurped Heket's position as wife of Khnum and became the second member of the Elephantine triad and goddess of the life-giving inundation. She was usually called the daughter of Ra, but sometimes was thought to be the daughter of Khnum and Anuket. From early times she was said to stand at the entrance to the Underworld and to use water from four vases to purify the pharaoh as he entered the kingdom of the dead. Later Satis became a goddess of hunting and was called Princess of Upper Egypt and, in the New Kingdom, Queen of the Gods.

She was represented wearing a vulture headdress and the white crown of Upper Egypt flanked by antelope horns, and she carried a bow and arrow; she was thus a Southern counterpart of Neith, another ancient goddess. Satis was often represented pouring out the waters of the Nile and spreading them over the land.

Anuket

Anuket (or Anukis) was originally a water-deity from the Sudan, whose cult centre was at the present Aswan. She was called the sister of Satis or sometimes her mother and became the concubine of Khnum and the third member of the Elephantine triad. Her name meant 'to embrace', which was taken to signify that her embrace during the inundation fertilised the fields. She became a goddess of lust, whose attributes and cult were obscene. Anuket was represented as a woman wearing a crown of feathers, perhaps those of a red parrot. She was at times identified with Nephthys.

Hapi

Hapi, god of the Nile and in particular of the inundation, was accorded universal devotion as bringer of fertility. His cult was considered vital and his special worshippers exalted him even above Ra. Hapi was said to water the meadows on which grazed the cattle of Ra, or mankind; to provide water in the desert oases; and to provide the dew from heaven (as we have seen, a river flowed through the heavens). Hapi was called the father of the gods, for he was the sustainer and lord of the gods of the earth, of fertility and of creation, providing the offerings made to them in their temples and hence nourishing men and supporting the divine order.

Hapi was identified with Nun and said to flow through the Duat, the Underworld, through the heavens, and through Egypt, after emerging in two whirlpools in the caverns of Elephantine. He lived on the island of Bigeh at the First Cataract of the Nile, where he could be found reclining on a couch in a grotto whose entrance was guarded by Khnum. Sometimes Hapi was considered as two gods – of the southern and of the northern Nile – who together performed the *samtaui* ritual, the unification of the Two Lands. Nekhebet was often thought to be Hapi's wife. At other times the single god Hapi represented both that part of the Nile which flowed north through Egypt and the other half of the waters which emerged at Elephantine and flowed south through Nubia.

As a fertility-god, Hapi was identified with Osiris, whose ritual obsequies were held annually at the height of the inundation. Alternatively, Hapi

Opposite. Min, god of fertility and bestower of human sexual powers, with whom the pharaoh was identified when he ritually begot his heir. Though of Lower Egyptian origin, in this bronze of the Late Period (c. 600 B.C.) his connection with his Upper Egyptian counterpart is seen in his wearing the feathers of Amon-Ra, while the solar disk derives equally from his earlier identification with Horus. He is brandishing a whip, derived from his early fetish, the thunderbolt. British Museum, London.

Above. Hapi, god of the Nile, with offering trays. Hapi's female breast symbolised his role as bringer of the flood which provided food for men and the gods. Relief on a sandstone pillar. Temple of Rameses II at Abydos.

was said to personify the waters of the Nile and Osiris their fertilising force. In Osirian belief the Nile waters were considered to be the sweat of Osiris's hands and the tears that Isis shed into the river were said to cause the annual flood. Hapi helped to resurrect Osiris by suckling him at his breast.

Hapi was represented as a bearded man coloured green or blue, with pendent female breasts to indicate his fertility. He wore a clump of water plants on his head – generally papyrus, but lotus when he was considered god of the Upper Nile. He was often depicted bearing heavily laden offering tables or pouring water libations from a vase. Sometimes he was shown holding two plants or two vases, which represented the Upper Nile and the Lower Nile.

Hapi should not be confused with Hapy, son of Horus, who was the tutelary deity of the Canopic jar containing the lungs.

Min

Min, whose cult centres were Chemmis in the Delta and Koptos, was a deity of predynastic origin whose fetish was a thunderbolt. In early times Min was considered to be a sky-god, a supreme being whose title was Chief of Heaven. Until well into the Middle Kingdom he was identified with the falcon-god Horus the Elder. He was called the son of Ra, or of Shu.

Min was above all a god of fertility, worshipped by men as a bestower of sexual powers. As a rain-god he also personified the generative force in nature, especially the growth immanent in grain. In representations of one of the important Min festivals, the pharaoh was shown hoeing the ground and watering the fields while Min looked on. At the Min festival held at the beginning of the harvest season, the pharaoh was seen ceremonially reaping the grain. In the Middle Kingdom Min was identified with Horus son of Osiris through this connection with the pharaoh as source of abundance. When he begot his heir (ritually at the same festival), the pharaoh was again identified with Min. As pharaohs were also said to

be the sons of Ra, Min came to be identified with the sun-god; and in the New Kingdom he was still more closely linked with Amon-Ra. At this period Min became a very popular deity and orgiastic festivals were held in his honour.

Despite his fertility associations, Min was well known as Lord of the Eastern Desert, for he was the tutelary deity of the caravan routes to the Red Sea which departed from Koptos, passing through dangerous tribal lands. He was called Lord of Foreign Lands and was the protector of nomads and hunters.

Min was represented as an ithyphallic bearded man, usually a statue with legs close together in the archaic fashion, painted black. He wore the same headdress as Amon, two tall feathers, and held one arm raised to brandish a scourge or a thunderbolt. In the New Kingdom he was shown presiding over the harvest festival in the form of his sacred animal, a white bull, which was often fed his special plant, the lettuce, believed to have aphrodisiac properties.

Bes

Bes came to Egypt in the Twelfth Dynasty from the Sudan, his foreign origin being shown by the fact that, unlike the other gods, he was represented full-face. He may originally have been a lion-god, for he retained some lion attributes, but in Egypt he was always depicted as a hideous dwarf or pygmy. At first he was a protector of the royal house, being for example one of the attendant deities at the birth of Hatshepsut. Later he was enthusiastically adopted by the common people and became one of the most popular deities.

Bes was the bringer of happiness to homes at all levels of society. He protected the family, presiding over marriage and the toilet and adornment of women. He was the greatest friend of women, helping them in childbirth and protecting the newborn child. He was often depicted dancing round the new mother while beating a small drum or tambourine and slashing about him with knives. This noise and menace, his ugliness, and the laughter

Above. Hapi Atur, god of the Nile of heaven. The Nile was thought to be a river or ocean encircling the universe. The heavenly Nile was the course of the sun during the daytime, while the infernal Nile flowed through the underworld to emerge at the First Cataract. Here Khnum acted as Hapi Atur's deputy. The river also flowed through the Nile valley, which to Egyptians was the universe. Musei Vaticani.

Opposite. Bes, depicted as a deformed dwarf in this statue, was none the less a popular deity. His image was often found in homes as a protection against danger, particularly from animals. Twenty-sixth Dynasty. Musée du Louvre, Paris.

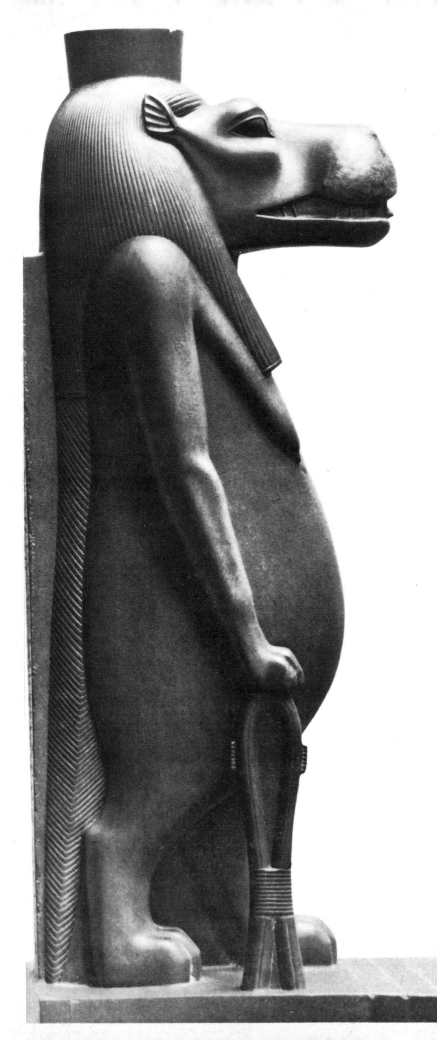

he provoked were intended to frighten away evil spirits.

Bes also protected his worshippers against noxious desert animals, especially snakes, and against other terrors. He was often shown strangling and devouring serpents. As destroyer of evil spirits, Bes came to be considered a powerful sorcerer. Though sometimes portrayed in military dress as slayer of his worshippers' enemies, he was primarily a god of good humour and of merry-making. He danced and played the harp and lyre as well as his tambourine in order to entertain the gods. In imitation of this, dancing and music-making were an important part of his cult.

Bes was represented as a dwarf with long arms, short bandy legs and a tail. His wide, snub-nosed face bore a shaggy beard and his huge eyes were half obscured by thick eyebrows. He had a large protruding tongue, projecting ears and sometimes had short horns growing from his forehead. Occasionally he wore a crown of tall plumes similar to that of Satis. His shaggy beard and brows were often described as leonine, and he was usually represented wearing the skin of a leopard or of a lion. Bes was most frequently depicted on bedheads, especially of marriage beds, or mirror handles, on perfume jars and on other domestic articles. He also figured on amulets made of hippopotamus ivory which were intended to give protection against desert animals and snakes. Finally, he became a protector and bringer of peace to the dead, being depicted on the pillows supporting the heads of mummies.

The female counterpart of Bes was Beset, a fire-spitting serpent; but Bes was more generally thought to be married to Taueret.

Taueret

Taueret (otherwise known as Thoeris and Apet) was a predynastic hippopotamus-deity, a mother-goddess whose name meant the 'Great One'. Sometimes she wore the solar disk and cow's horns, a reminder that she assisted at the daily rebirth of the sun. She was even called the Eye of

Right. Seker, the necropolis deity of Memphis, as a mummified hawk wearing the *atef* crown of Osiris. From the Papyrus of Ani, a version of the *Book of the Dead*. Nineteenth Dynasty, c. 1250 B.C. British Museum, London.

Opposite. Taueret, goddess of childbirth. Usually represented as a pregnant hippopotamus standing on the hind legs of a lion and with the tail of a crocodile. She rests her hand on a plait of rolled papyrus which forms the symbol for protection, *sa.* Twenty-sixth Dynasty. From her temple at Karnak.

Ra, his daughter, and the mother of Isis and Osiris.

Gradually Taueret became an inferior deity in the official religion; but she was feared as well as revered as a domestic deity. At all periods and at all levels of society Taueret was the protectress of women in pregnancy and childbirth. Thus in the Eighteenth Dynasty she was often shown with Bes dancing around her in the birth chamber; and she was a prominent assistant at the birth of Hatshepsut.

Amulets of Taueret as well as of Bes were placed in tombs, so that she might protect the rebirth of the deceased into the kingdom of the dead. As she was sometimes considered the wife of Set, however, she later acquired an evil reputation.

Taueret was represented as a pregnant female hippopotamus with pendent human breasts, standing on her hind legs, which were those of a lioness; she had the tail of a crocodile. She was usually depicted leaning against the symbol for protection and carrying that of life. Taueret had temples at Thebes and at Deir el-Bahri, the site of Hatshepsut's tomb.

Meshkent

Meshkent, goddess of childbirth, was sometimes considered as four deities, goddesses of the birth chamber, the birth stool and the two birth bricks on which Egyptian women crouched when the child was delivered. These goddesses and other birth-deities appeared to women at the moment of delivery, sometimes in the form of dancing-girls who celebrated with music in the birth chamber. Meshkent, or the four Meshkents, were said to be married to Shai, and could predict the destiny of the child at the moment of birth. Meshkent predicted a glorious future when she presided at the birth of Hatshepsut.

Like other birth-deities, Meshkent was also associated with the rebirth after death. She assisted Isis and Nephthys in the funerary rites; equally, Isis and Nephthys became connected through this association with the birth of kings on earth, Isis receiving the baby. Finally, Meshkent testified as to the character of the deceased at the judgement before Osiris.

Meshkent was represented as a woman wearing on her head two high plumes coiled at the tips, which have been interpreted as palm shoots or as a tall water-plant. She was also represented as the birth brick itself, which was given a woman's head.

Renenet

Renenet (or Renenutet) was a nurse-goddess who presided over suckling, assisting and protecting every child at birth. She thus became closely associated with the idea of destiny in the sense of good fortune and riches. In this aspect she was early confused and merged with Ernutet, originally a personification of the rich harvest, who was identified with the cobra which often hid in the ripe corn.

Renenet had associations with Meshkent and also with Mayet and Sebek. She was represented as a woman with the head of a cobra, generally the royal *uraeus*, and wearing a headdress consisting of two plumes or of the solar disk and a pair of cow's horns. She was often depicted suckling the pharaoh and sometimes the souls of the deceased.

Shai

Shai, whose name meant 'What is ordained', was the personification of destiny or luck, and in general thought to be a beneficent 'guardian angel' attached to each man at the moment of birth. But Shai could also be a portent of misfortunes, especially after Renenet became 'good fortune'. Through Shai was also ordained the length of life allotted and the nature of the man's eventual death.

In the New Kingdom Shai was considered the husband of Meshkent, and like her was present at the birth and at the judgement of the dead. Shai was not absolutely inalterable: man could affect his destiny by his actions in life, and the gods could affect it too. But he was inescapable: he accompanied a man from the moment of birth to the judgement hall of Osiris, where he bore witness as to the character of the man; if the soul was 'justified', Shai led it into the life after death.

Shai was represented as a man in early times; then as a goat; and finally as a serpent. Often he was depicted beneath the birth brick with the woman's head, Meshkent.

The Hathors

Egyptian deities could have seven or nine forms: Hathor adopted seven forms in her aspect as the mother-goddess who lived in the Tree of Heaven and nourished the souls of men. The Seven Hathors performed this office for the deceased and for the newborn. It was they who at the birth of each child announced his fate, generally calling this Shai, but identifying it with Renenet if it was particularly favourable.

The Hathors were usually represented as a group of young women playing upon tambourines and wearing the disk and horns of Hathor. In Ptolemaic times they were identified with the Pleiades.

Hu, Sia, Sehem and Heh

The abstract qualities which enabled creation to occur and to be sustained were deified. The most important were Hu, Sia, Sehem and Heh, or Neheh.

Hu and Sia, whom we have already met as members of the crew in Ra's solar barque, were represented as bearded men and personified respectively Command or Authoritative Utterance, the motive force behind creation; and Intelligence, whereby the work of creation was executed. Sia, Intelligence, was closely associated with Thoth, god of wisdom and divine artificer. Hu and Sia also served as bearers of the Eye of Horus. Originally aspects of Ra's creative power, Hu and Sia were considered in Memphis to personify the Tongue and Heart of Ptah. It was through the heart that men related their lives to moral precepts: thus Sia was conscience and character.

Sehem, Energy, was also an essential force in creation, while Heh, Eternity, and his female counterpart Hehet were aspects of Nun, the primeval ocean, personifying infinite space. Heh was represented as a man wearing a curved reed on his head, squatting and carrying the traditional symbols of long life and happiness. He became popular in later times as a domestic deity.

Mayet

Mayet was the goddess of truth, of justice and of reality. She symbolised the balance between the antitheses in Egyptian life: between Upper and Lower Egypt; between the fertile valley and the desert; and so between good and evil. She was thus the basis of civilisation and Egyptian strength.

Mayet was said to reign when the kingdom was unified and when men were peaceful and content with their lot, performing their duties of righteous conduct as laid down in the divine order. Without Mayet creation could not be sustained and the divine intention was thwarted. The pharaoh was the chief upholder of Mayet, and when he could present her to the gods he was giving them the most precious thing, sometimes offered instead of the ritual meal. For the gods themselves lived by Mayet. She was said to be the daughter of Ra and the wife of Thoth, having accompanied them in the solar barque when they emerged from Nun for the first time,

before creation of the world. The light which Ra brought to the world was Mayet: he created the world by putting her in the place of chaos. She was therefore always depicted as one of the crew of the solar barque.

All the pharaohs claimed to rule by Mayet, including Akhenaten; but his successors asserted that his reign had toppled her, for it was not conducted according to the tradition said to derive from the reign of Horus on earth. The proof of this was that the kingdom became weak and much of the empire was lost. The successors made much of re-establishing Mayet in her rightful place, thus restoring equilibrium among the gods as well as on earth.

The ordinary people were called on to sustain Mayet more than the other royal gods. They did not have to wait for the democratisation of beliefs about the afterlife to be affected by her through the pharaoh, the priesthood and the laws of the land: all judges were called her priests. But she

Porcelain figures of the four sons of Horus, divine guardians of the four cardinal points and of the Canopic jars: *left to right* jackal-headed Duamutef, falcon-headed Qebehsenuf, human-headed Imset and dog-headed Hapy. Such figurines were buried with the deceased when separate embalmment of the viscera in jars was discontinued. Nineteenth Dynasty.

later became still more important to them for her role in the judgement hall of Osiris. She ushered the soul of the deceased into the hall. Then her figure was placed in one pan of the balance while the heart of the deceased was placed in the other. If the pans balanced the heart was said to be justified, to be 'true of voice' – in other words, it fitted into its allotted place in the divine order.

Mayet was represented as a woman standing in the solar barque or seated on a throne in the Osirian hall of judgement and wearing a tall ostrich feather on her head. Alternatively she was represented by the feather alone, especially during the judgement ritual, when it was weighed against the heart of the deceased.

Divinities of Death

The Osirian deities absorbed most of the ancient gods connected with death, and the Osirian system caused many deities of birth to be associated with the Underworld through rebirth after death. These we have already discussed. Nevertheless a certain number of deities retained their primary character as funerary gods and were never absorbed by and were little involved in the mythology of the great gods.

Seker

Seker (or Sokaris) was an early fetish deity of Memphis, and took the form of a sparrow-hawk. He became the god of the Memphite necropolis on the western bank of the Nile, for he was a deity of darkness and decay in the earth. He was called the soul of Geb. The sandy desert was the Underworld kingdom of Seker, and in order to cross it Ra's boat had to be turned into a serpent, which was represented with sledge-runners. The principal shrine of Seker was called 'Gate of the Ways' (Ro-Setau), for he stood at the entrance to his kingdom in order to feed upon the hearts of the dead. He was represented as a hawk or as a hawk-headed mummy.

Seker was identified with Osiris as early as the Old Kingdom. He was also identified with Ptah of Memphis, and the three gods were combined in a triad or composite deity called Ptah-Seker-Osiris. This deity was at first depicted as a pygmy with short thick limbs and a large bald head on which he wore horns and plumes, or a scarab representing the creative powers of Khepri; the figure may have been intended as a human foetus. In the Late Period, when Osiris was thought to be incarnate in a bull, Ptah-Seker-Osiris was also represented in that form.

Selket

Selket (or Serquet) was a scorpion-goddess who seems to have been honoured by a predynastic king known as King Scorpion. She had fertility associations, for she was one of the protective goddesses of the four sources of the Nile. Her connection with these exits from the Underworld, the infernal ocean, led to her gradual relegation to the Underworld as kingdom of the dead. When Apep had been defeated by the defenders of Ra, he was bound and kept in the Underworld, where Selket was appointed to guard him. She was made the consort of Nekhebkau, a serpent-deity with human limbs who was sometimes considered one of the monsters inhabiting the Underworld; Selket was then said to bind the dead with chains. But her husband was at other times considered a beneficent deity who provided food to sustain the souls of the dead; in this case Selket too became a friendly deity.

Selket was most commonly described as helping Isis in performing the funerary rites for Osiris and as assisting her in looking after the infant Horus. She stood with Isis at the foot of coffins and was the tutelary deity of one of the Canopic jars.

Selket was represented as a woman with a scorpion on her head or as a scorpion with a woman's head. Sometimes, like Isis, she protected the dead with winged arms.

Mertseger

Mertseger was called Mistress of the West, that is of the kingdom of the dead, the land of the setting sun. Her name meant 'Beloved of him who makes silence' (Osiris), and she in fact symbolised the Theban necropolis. Another of her titles was Peak of the West, for she lived on a steep mountain which rose a thousand feet above the Valley of the Kings, where the pharaohs of the New Kingdom were buried in rock-tombs. Mertseger was described as the lion of the summit, for she was fierce in the pursuit of sin, punishing with illness and ultimately with death those who failed to pay her due respect. To the just, however, she was a beneficent deity, particularly potent in the protection she gave against serpents. Mertseger was perhaps an aspect of the *uraeus* serpent, fierce in its protective aspects, but originally the instrument of death for the pharaoh. She was sometimes represented as a cobra, and sometimes as a woman with a cobra's head.

The four sons of Horus

Horus had a number of wives and a numerous progeny, but those who were grouped together as his 'four sons' were generally said to be his offspring by Isis. They were born from a lotus flower, for they had originally been sons of Horus the Elder and therefore solar gods belonging to the legends of creation. They were retrieved from the water by Sebek, on the orders of Ra. They were also called the sons of Geb, or the sons of Atum and Nut, and it was said that they 'never saw corruption'. In Osirian belief therefore Anubis charged them with the duties of mummification, with the Opening of the Mouth, and with the burial first of Osiris, and then of men in general. Horus later appointed them to be guardians of the four cardinal points.

The four sons of Horus were most commonly imagined as the guardians of the Canopic jars, the four vessels in which the viscera of the deceased were placed, having been removed before the embalmment of the body. The jars themselves were closely identified with the four tutelary goddesses which watched over the body. Thus Isis was associated with the jar containing the liver, which was guarded by Imset, the man-headed son of Horus who also represented the south. Nephthys was associated with the jar containing the lungs, which was guarded by the ape- or dog-headed Hapy, who represented the north. Neith was associated with the jar containing the stomach, guarded by Duamutef, who was the jackal-headed representative of the east. And Selket was identified with the jar containing the intestines.

Until the Eighteenth Dynasty these jars had human-headed stoppers; but thereafter each stopper represented the head of the appropriate son of Horus. Still later, the viscera were no longer removed, but mummy-shaped figurines with the heads of the four sons of Horus were buried with the deceased. The four played a part in the Underworld too, and were often depicted standing on an open lotus flower before the throne of Osiris in the hall of judgement.

Men Deified and the Divine Pharaoh

Imhotep

Imhotep was the vizier of Djoser, the first, or perhaps the second, pharaoh of the Third Dynasty, whose capital was Memphis. Like a number of subsequent viziers, Imhotep was skilled in many branches of administration and indeed in all the fields of royal enterprise. His fame rested not only on his talents, however, but also on the fact that he was original, the first man other than a pharaoh to leave his imprint on the history of Egyptian civilisation. He was famed as a priest learned in Heliopolitan doctrine; as a writer; as a physician; and above all as a scholar who contributed to

the founding of the disciplines of astronomy and architecture. He was known to Egyptians of all ages as the architect of the Step Pyramid or mastaba of Djoser at Saqqara, near Memphis. This monument, in whose precincts were many smaller buildings to be used in ritual by the king, was constructed of limestone blocks faced with white stone from Tura, on the east bank of the Nile. It was the first building ever to be made entirely of stone, and with it Egyptian civilisation came of age.

The building of temples and funerary monuments was of course a sacred undertaking, and it was as a wise man and scribe that Imhotep was first honoured. In the New Kingdom he was regarded as patron of scribes, who poured a few drops of water in

libation to him before beginning to write. It seems that a form of ancestor-worship was privately practised from the New Kingdom onwards, and the cult of Imhotep was similar to that of the dead. At this time he was identified with Nefertum.

In the Saite Period Imhotep was fully deified, being called the son of Ptah by a lady name Khroti-onkh, or by Nut, or by Sekhmet; he replaced Nefertum in the triad of Memphis, where a temple was erected to him. He was associated particularly with Ptah and Thoth and became patron of wisdom, especially of medicine in the form of magic exorcism, miraculous cures being ascribed to him. The Greeks identified him with Asclepius, and he was a popular god under the Ptolemies, especially Euergetes II. He was represented without divine insignia, as a priest with a shaven head, seated and holding on his knees an open papyrus roll. Sometimes he was clothed in the archaic dress of a priest.

Amenhotep

Amenhotep son of Hapu was vizier at the court of Amenhotep III in the Eighteenth Dynasty. Officially, his chief concern was with military affairs, but he was the architect of many monuments on an enormous scale. Amenhotep III spent most of his reign engaged in building.

Like Imhotep, Amenhotep was revered because he represented the body of tradition. He was known as a learned man who had been 'shown all the sacred books and beheld the excellencies of Thoth'. He was a sage counsellor and was said to have written a book of magic, thus showing his participation in the divine nature of Thoth.

His cult was established in his lifetime by decree of Amenhotep III, who dedicated a statue to him in his temple at Karnak and provided mortuary revenues for him in perpetuity in his own tomb on the west bank of the Nile at Thebes. Ptolemy IV built a temple at Deir el-Medina round Amenhotep's grave, which was already considered sacred. In this temple Amenhotep and Imhotep were worshipped together, in the company of the gods. Amenhotep, who was especially associated with Osiris and Amon-Ra, was also worshipped at Karnak. He was represented as a bearded man holding a papyrus roll.

Pharaohs as Gods

The pharaoh may have been regarded as a living god in the early Old Kingdom, when the monarchy was associated with Horus cults. The king as rain-maker was the foundation of all; and as lord of hunters and warriors he was thought in the afterlife to hunt and eat the gods as he hunted game on earth. From the Fifth Dynasty onwards, however, with the rise of Heliopolis, the pharaoh became only the son of a god – though for the purposes of ritual he kept his traditional status and when visiting their shrines treated all gods except Ra as his equals. He was their living representative on earth and at the same time their priest, so he was sometimes portrayed worshipping himself, or purifying the gods in the same way as they purified him at his birth and accession – to preserve his divine nature. The pharaoh was commonly called 'creator of all things' and the 'Eye of Ra'. The difference between gods and king was less than that be-

tween king and subjects; nevertheless the pharaoh had to rely on the good-will of Ra and his ferryman to reach the afterlife at all. There, if accepted, he acted as Ra's secretary or as one of the crew of the solar barque.

The prestige of the pharaohs was undermined by military and economic weakness and by admixtures of commoners' blood in the royal house. The distance between the king and the notables and provincial governors grew less as the latter aspired to the afterlife and built themselves independent domains on earth and private funerary monuments away from the royal burial grounds. These potentates also proved their personal worth by their achievements as scholars and artists – the men who actually ran the kingdom. In fact the aspirations of most of these officials were based on some blood relationship to the pharaoh, which made some part of his divine nature latent in them.

Meanwhile the growing popularity of Osirian beliefs and the resultant identification of the pharaoh with this archetypal king led to the clear distinction between the living pharaoh, who had divine blood, and the pharaoh after death, when he might hope to become a god, one with Osiris. The distinction was made clear in the use

Above. Imhotep, the architect of the Step Pyramid, which he built to house the tomb of his master, the Third-Dynasty pharaoh Djoser. Imhotep was deified by later generations and venerated for his wisdom and learning. He is shown dressed as a priest and, as patron of scribes, with a roll of papyrus.

Opposite. Painted limestone block statue of Amenhotep the son of Hapu. He was scribe and vizier to the pharaoh Amenhotep III and honoured greatly in life and death. Though he never became a true god divine honours were paid to his memory. Thebes. Eighteenth Dynasty.

Left. Painted lid of the sarcophagus of Soter, archon of Thebes. Horus on the left and Thoth on the right perform the lustral ceremonies which imbued the pharaohs with their divine authority. Second century A.D. British Museum, London.

Above. The protective scorpion-deity Selket at one corner of the gilded wooden shrine of Tutankhamon. Selket guarded one of the four gates of the Underworld, and so was a goddess of fertility and of the afterlife. Egyptian Museum, Cairo.

Opposite. A coloured relief of Rameses II in the Great Temple at Abu Simbel. The pharaoh is being embraced by a goddess, probably Isis. The subject-matter of the reliefs at Abu Simbel and the scale of the undertaking were designed in part to impress on the subject Nubians the divine power of their suzerain.

of 'good god' to refer to the pharaoh and of 'great god' to refer to the heavenly deities. After death pharaohs were gods by assimilation to Ra or Osiris rather than in their own characters. In the same way any man who was drowned in the Nile was identified with Osiris and could be deified. When the people wished to worship a king they worshipped Osiris, Amon-Ra or Ra-Harakhte.

Until Ptolemaic times no pharaohs actually received worship in their lifetime – though there were occasions when their funerary temples were completed before their death and the cult was immediately begun in them. After their death, however, certain pharaohs were accorded worship beyond the funerary ritual in which the dead pharaoh was equated with the great gods. Such were Amenhotep I and Amenhotep III, Thuthmosis III and Rameses II, all of whom were known as great builders of temples. Half the temples seen today in Egypt date from the reign of Rameses II.

Amenhotep I was worshipped in conjunction with his mother Ahmes-Nefertari. They were considered the patron deities of the necropolis to the west of Thebes, for he was the first pharaoh to be buried in a rock-tomb at some distance from the mortuary temple in the Theban plain below. He had gathered craftsmen together at this new necropolis and given them their livelihood; consequently he was credited with miraculous protective powers, for example saving one of them from death when he had thrust his hand into a hole where a poisonous snake was lurking. Some of these workmen were of foreign origin or in contact with foreigners accustomed to such cults; but in fact Amenhotep I was also worshipped by native priests and officials at Thebes and throughout Egypt. He was particularly venerated in the form of two statues not in his mortuary temple, called Amenhotep of the Forecourt and Amenhotep the Favourite (of Amon); he was represented as a bearded man with black flesh.

Amenhotep III was worshipped in conjunction with his wife, Tiy, in several places but especially at Thebes in Greek and Roman times. The Greeks identified him with their hero-deity Memnon, whose colossal statue was a famous monument at Thebes, for until about A.D. 200 it 'sang' at sunrise. This statue had in fact been

erected by Amenhotep III, and was one of a pair which adorned the gate of his funerary temple.

The Sacred Animals

Though tribal fetishes in predynastic times often took the form of animals, these creatures were not really gods. Animals were not generally treated as gods until later times and then only when they had been personified, usually as the embodiment of some god's soul. Even then only an individual animal was worshipped, though exaggerated respect was certainly shown to all members of the species.

Animal-worship increased as the cult of the god incarnate in the king decreased: the popular imagination needed a tangible representative of the deities. The common people acquired merit in tending the animals, just as they had previously justified

themselves by fulfilling their obligations towards the law as embodied in the king and thus upholding the divine order of Mayet. Veneration of animals also grew in proportion as foreign influence increased, for the priests encouraged it, recognising that the divine association with animals was the most characteristically Egyptian feature of their ancient religion.

It was said that an early king had ordered the worship of animals; or that Isis had instituted worship of the animals which had helped Osiris – and abomination of those which had attacked him; or that when men became unruly, the gods for fear of them took refuge in the forms of animals.

Animal cults formerly devoted privately by simple people now became the prerogative of the state itself, which provided impressive funerals for the more important animal deities such as Apis or Mnevis. This lead

encouraged more elaborate private devotional practices. It became customary to try to bury all animals of a species in the city where their chosen representative was specially honoured. For example cats, sometimes carefully mummified, would be taken to the special cat-cemetery at Bubastis, while a dead ibis would be taken for burial to Hermopolis. Bulls would be buried at the place of their death, but their horns were left protruding from the ground: pious inhabitants of Atarbekhis in the Delta would scour the kingdom looking for these horns, which they would pull out and take home for reburial. Cows would be thrown into the holy Nile, a way of ensuring their deification (through identification with Osiris and because Apis was a form of the Nile).

Just as some gods were not beneficent, so there were evil animal spirits. Such were snakes in some guises; the

animals associated with Set, such as the black pig, the crocodile and the hippopotamus; and, of the Nile creatures, the *oxyrhyncus* – the Nile crab which ate the phallus of Osiris. These animals were not, however, universally abhorred: in some cities they were worshipped – especially the hippopotamus and the crocodile. This situation led to fierce warfare between cities, for the deliberate killing of sacred animals became a capital offence, and accidental killings were punished by severe fines. Killing an ibis or a falcon was in every case punished by death.

Sacred Bulls

Mnevis

Mnevis (in Egyptian, Nemur) was a bull worshipped as the 'living sun-god Ra' at Heliopolis. His life was said to repeat the life of Ra, and later that of Osiris, at every stage of the cycle. The bull is of course a universal fertility symbol and we have frequently in the solar mythology come across Kamephis, 'Bull of his Mother', in connection with the daily birth, death and rebirth from his own seed of the heavenly calf, the sun. The name Kamephis seems to be connected with the *ka*, the vital principle of a man or of a god; Kamephis, the bull, was said to embody the soul, or the creative energy of certain gods. In the same way the pharaoh, giver of fertility to his kingdom, was often referred to as a bull. The Mnevis bull was probably worshipped in predynastic times at Heliopolis, though according to tradition his cult was instituted in the Second Dynasty. He was worshipped by all kings, including Akhenaten.

The Mnevis bull lived in a temple at Heliopolis and was a black or occasionally a piebald animal with massive shoulders – of a different breed from Apis. In artistic representations he was shown wearing the sun-disk and *uraeus*.

Apis

Apis (in Egyptian, Hapi) was a form of the Nile-god; in other words he was another fertility-deity. His cult as the bull of Heliopolis was supposed to have been established by Menes or by the first king of the Second Dynasty. In fact it existed in predynastic times and continued in various forms throughout the pharaonic period. At Memphis Apis was worshipped as the 'renewed life of Ptah' or as Ptah's 'double' or 'deputy'. It was said that he dwelt in the soul of Ptah.

He was later known as an incarnation of the son of Osiris, and was called the 'life of Osiris', who 'gives life, health and strength to the nostrils of the king'. Osiris was in fact connected with Apis in predynastic times, when Osiris was allied with bull-peoples in the Delta; it was then that he acquired the title 'Bull of Ament' (the Underworld). The later association of Apis and Osiris derived especially from the creation, death and resurrection triad of Ptah-Seker-Osiris. Osiris-Apis became known as Serapis or Sarapis. In an attempt to associate the popular cult of Osiris

with that of Ra, the Heliopolitan priests put forward the notion that when the Apis bull died his soul rose to heaven to be united with that of Osiris; Serapis was therefore a sort of heaven-god. Nevertheless he was also known as a god of the Underworld and particularly of the riches beneath the earth. The Greeks easily identified him with Hades. He was, however, also associated with Atum and the various moon-gods.

The Apis bull was said to be engendered by a ray of light descending on and fertilising a cow who was incapable of bearing another calf. There were in all twenty-nine separate distinguishing marks, and a special priest was appointed to search the land for a bull bearing all of them. The bull was black, and the best known of the marks were a triangular white patch on the forehead (Herodotus thought it was square); an eagle on the back; double hairs in the tail; and a scarab on the tongue. According to Herodotus all Egypt rejoiced when a new Apis was found and everyone put on festive clothing.

When the new bull was found the old one was put to death ceremonially by drowning in the Nile. The flesh may have been eaten, while the skin, bones and other parts of the body were mummified, given royal funerary rites, including the provision of human *ushabtis*, and was buried with great pomp at Saqqara. The burial vault or Serapeum was an underground structure begun in the Eighteenth Dynasty, where the lives of all the bulls were carefully recorded. There were twenty-four Apis bulls between the reign of Rameses II and the first of the Ptolemies, and a total of sixty were buried at Saqqara.

Rejoicing over the discovery of the new bull gave way to sixty days of deep mourning for the old one (this compared with seventy days for a pharaoh). The pious were expected to eat nothing but vegetables and water during this time. The bull was embalmed in the most precious oils and placed in a coffin made of the choicest woods. In 547 B.C. Amasis, a pharaoh of the Twenty-sixth Dynasty, built a red granite sarcophagus for the

deceased Apis bull, more splendid than any that had ever been made for a king. The mummified bull was adorned with gold and precious stones. This was the first of the great bull-sarcophagi at Saqqara.

The living Apis bull was kept in a court by the southern gateway of the sanctuary of Ptah at Memphis. There he was enthroned and honoured with many festivals; his advice was sought on numerous matters, for he was thought to have oracular powers. In artistic representations he was shown as a bull wearing the sun-disk and *uraeus* or as a bull-headed man standing with his legs apart, wearing the moon-disk within the crescent moon and two large plumes. He wore a breastplate on which were two cobras and he carried the royal insignia of Osiris.

The chief cult centre of Apis was moved to Alexandria under Ptolemy I Soter who, when he was pondering which god could be made the national deity, had a dream in which he saw a statue of a bull-god. He had never seen such a god before, but his councillors advised him that there was one like it at Sinope. Ptolemy ordered it to be brought to Alexandria, but the Sinopians refused to part with it; after three years of argument, the statue moved itself to Alexandria, making a three-day voyage. Ptolemy built a new Serapeum for it there. The cult spread to Athens and other parts of the Greek empire, and finally to Rome.

Buchis

Buchis (also known as Bacis and Bkha) was the third famous bull-deity. His cult centre was at Hermonthis, where he was said to be the incarnation of the lord of the city, the warrior-god Mont, who was called the 'strong bull'. Buchis was famed for his strength, violence and pugnacity. He was also identified with Osiris and called the 'Living soul of Ra' and the 'Bull of the Mountains of Sunrise and Sunset'. He was a black bull, but the colour of his hair changed every hour of the day. The figure of a vulture could be seen on his back. He was represented wearing on his head

The Bennu bird, a huge golden hawk with heron's head, the form in which, according to Heliopolitan tradition, Ra-Atum alighted at dawn on the Benben, a sun-ray obelisk, to disperse the inchoate darkness of Nun. In token of this assertion of renewed life and order, the deceased greeted the Bennu bird on arrival in the heavenly afterlife. From the tomb of Anhurkhawi at Thebes. Twentieth Dynasty.

the solar disk and *uraeus* between two plumes, and was often smelling a lotus flower. He was of late origin, the first mention of him occurring during the reign of Nectanebo II of the Thirtieth Dynasty, the last native pharaoh.

Other bull-deities included the Golden Bull of Canopus, near Alexandria; the bull of Min; the bull of the sky, son and husband of Nut; and the bull of Mayet. Cows too were sacred, being identified with Hathor, Nut and Isis.

Sacred Rams

Apart from the ram-deities Khnum, Harsaphes and Amon, actual rams were worshipped in many cities for their strength, virility and energy, and especially at Hermopolis, Lycopolis and Mendes or Busiris. The Ram of Mendes, Banebdetet, was the most famous, and was made one of the arbiters in the great quarrel of Horus and Set. As the bulls were connected with the *ka*, so this ram was connected with the *ba*. His name meant 'Soul, Lord of Busiris'. This was equated with the soul of Osiris. Later the Ram of Mendes was given four heads, which represented the souls of Ra, Shu, Geb and Osiris. He was also connected with Ptah, who took his form to create Rameses II. His wife was a dolphin-goddess, Hat-mehit.

The Ram of Mendes was buried with pomp and great mourning, at public expense. He was especially honoured by Ptolemy II, who rebuilt his temple and enthroned in it two rams. He was represented as a ram with horizontal wavy horns, sometimes wearing the *uraeus* on his head and sometimes enthroned.

Above. A realistic statue of Apis, the sacred bull in whom Osiris was believed to be incarnate. A granite carving of the Thirtieth Dynasty, from the Serapeum at Saqqara, near Memphis. Sixty-four mummified bulls were discovered here in 1851. Musée du Louvre, Paris.

Opposite. A wood carving of an ibis. Fitzwilliam Museum, Cambridge.

Sacred Crocodiles

The most famous of the sacred crocodiles was the one in which Sebek manifested himself, which was kept in Lake Moeris in the Faiyum. The priests decked its forelegs and ears with gold jewellery and precious stones and it was fed the choicest foods by the pilgrims who flocked to the sanctuary. His acceptance of food was a sign of his benevolence to the pilgrim. The supreme honour for a man was to fall into the Nile and be eaten by a crocodile.

Sacred Birds

The most famous of these was the Bennu bird, an imaginary bird rather like a heron. It was the incarnation of the sun as it appeared at the moment of creation alighting on the Benben stone, and was created from the fire burning at dawn on the sacred persea tree at Heliopolis; alternatively it sprang from the heart of Osiris. It was represented as a huge golden hawk with a heron's head, so that the Greeks identified the Bennu bird with the phoenix, a sort of eagle with red and gold wings. According to Herodotus, the Bennu bird was born in the pastures of the temple; but it was rarely seen there, for it appeared only every five hundred years, bringing the body of its recently deceased father to the temple in an egg made of myrrh.

Of real birds, the hawk was the most sacred, being identified with Horus son of Atum or Ra, and associated with the *ba* in the form of a human-headed hawk. Sparrowhawks were kept in the precincts of the sun-temples. The ibis, bird of Thoth, was worshipped at the Ibeum to the north of Hermopolis. Certain geese were said to be incarnations of Geb and Amon-Ra, while swallows were sacred to Isis, for this was the form in which she flew round the tamarisk tree enclosing Osiris's coffin at Byblos.

Other Animals

Innumerable other animals were given divine honours. Perhaps the most important were cats, who were sacred to Bast at Bubastis and elsewhere revered as killers of serpents. The cat-goddess Mafdet, 'Lady of the Castle of Life', was worshipped for this as early as the First Dynasty; and Ra took the form of a cat to strike off the head of Apep. The ichneumon was revered as slayer of snakes and eater of crocodile eggs; called Shed, he was the incarnation of Atum, the setting sun. A lion was worshipped at Leontopolis, while his wife Mehit or Mai-hesa ('fierce-eyed'), a lynx, was worshipped at Bubastis. They were identified with Anhur and Tefnut. A leopard was worshipped in the Sudan, for it was said to be possessed by the spirits of robbers, greatly feared on the edge of the desert. At Hermopolis they worshipped in addition to the ibis a hare which was thought to be a form of Ra or of Osiris. At Cynopolis a dog and a jackal, identified with Anubis, were worshipped. At Lycopolis or Asyut the animal worshipped was a wolf, which was identified with Upuaut and with Horus and Set, who once lived at Asyut in the form of wolves. Finally, the scarab was worshipped as incarnation of the rising sun, Khepri; while the cobra was identified with the *uraeus*, the Eye of Ra and so with Edjo or Buto. It was therefore associated with actions of protection, but actions achieved by fearsome, destructive means.

Life after Death: the Spread of the Osiris Cult

The Egyptian religion was one whose creed was not laid down in a rigid formula, but was open to constant reinterpretation through cult and usage, and this in turn depended in part on external political or historical influences. As a religion embodied in the cult rather than in the doctrine, it could keep alive only through the constant search of its followers for new interpretations. It therefore adapted itself to the needs of the times and to the needs of the particular worshipper. The search for new symbols went on constantly: each one was considered to represent one facet of the truth and did not necessarily entail rejection of previously held concepts. Equally, as the symbols changed, so shifts of emphasis could occur over the centuries as to the interpretation of the myths.

The modern reader must constantly bear in mind that the Egyptian myths, unlike the Greek or the Roman, cannot be considered as fixed stories. Their function in the Egyptian religion was to provide a notation of symbols with which to express ideas; if the ideas changed, then the myth also had to change. No myth is a better illustration of this principle than that of Osiris, which during the course of history underwent almost a complete reversal – of significance if not altogether of form.

The Beginnings of the Osiris Cult

From what we can guess of his origin, we suppose that Osiris was at first the fetish of a conquering clan which installed its god at Djedu, in the centre of the Delta region of Lower Egypt. This city was later named after him Per-Usire (Greek, Busiris). In Djedu, Osiris took the place of the former Lord of the City, Andjeti, a god associated with fertility cults and represented in human form as a king with the royal insignia of a long crooked sceptre and a whip in his hands and with two feathers on his head. Identification of Osiris with Andjeti was facilitated by the fact that both were always represented as human beings. Osiris soon took the name Andjeti as an epithet and became known as 'Lord of Djedu'.

In the earliest times the king was credited with the power to influence or control natural phenomena, simply because of his own great power. In later periods, the king was merely considered the intermediary between the gods, particularly the sun-god, and human beings. As such he was their only hope of securing the benevolence of the gods of nature and the benefits which they could confer. As we have already seen, the kings were ritually identified in the solar doctrines as 'sons of Ra'. In either case, the benefits which the king brought to his land were benefits of nature.

As recounted in the earlier discussion of the myth, Osiris was originally supposed to have been an actual king of Egypt, and some Egyptologists think that this may be historically true. In that case, he would naturally transfer to his deified character the attributes of a fertility-god. Whether it was because of this royal derivation or whether it was because of identification with Andjeti, who was always depicted as a living king and a god of fertility, Osiris was in fact associated with fertility cults from a very early stage. It seems, however,

that as early as the period of the *Pyramid Texts* Osiris was primarily a god of the dead. It was not until a much later stage, when he had usurped some of Ra's functions, and he and his son Horus had become the chief deities with which the pharaohs identified themselves, that the fertility associations were again to acquire any great importance.

Osiris as King of the Dead

In the earliest stages of his development in the historical period, therefore, Osiris was firmly fixed as a god of the dead. Though represented as a king, he was always shown as a dead king – a mummy bearing the royal insignia. His cult spread rapidly into Upper Egypt and he became identified with the funerary god of Abydos, Khenti-Amentiu, who was represented as a wolf. Osiris now became known as Osiris Khenti-Amentiu, 'Lord of the Westerners'. The 'West' to the Egyptians was the abode of the dead, as it was of the setting sun, and the 'Westerners' were therefore the dead.

Though the original cult centre of Osiris was at Busiris, in the Delta, a more important centre grew up at Abydos, in Upper Egypt, where the tomb was found of a king of the First Dynasty, Djer, whose name was misread as 'Khent'. It was believed that this was the tomb of Osiris himself. A further legend connecting Osiris with Abydos related that Isis found her husband's head there. A local fetish of Abydos found on monuments consisted of the remains of this head, set on a pole and adorned with a wig, feathers and horns. Abydos became a favoured burial ground; or in lieu of actual burial at Abydos, the Egyptians frequently had stelas erected there for the benefit of their departed.

As well as absorbing the gods Khenti-Amentiu and Andjeti, Osiris became identified with Seker, the god of the Memphite necropolis at Giza.

Osiris was imagined as a king of the dead; his province as a god did not therefore at first seem to encroach in any way on the preserves of the other gods, who were seen as being concerned with creation and, through the pharaoh's identification with the cult of the sun-god, with the order of the present world. The spread of the cult of Osiris as a funerary god was not seriously opposed by the priests of Heliopolis. Ra remained the supreme god, but Osiris, Isis and Horus, their child, were incorporated in the family of Ra, the solar pantheon.

Osiris's sphere was quite clearly delimited as a minor god of another world. He did not even in the early stages have supremacy in the world of the dead, for Ra was the most important figure in the Underworld as

well as in the heavens. In the form of Auf, the dead sun, he journeyed every night through the twelve provinces of the Underworld, speaking to the souls of the dead, admonishing those souls which were evil, shedding light and encouragement on the good souls, curing their pains, driving away their sorrows. He opened their nostrils and allowed them to breathe; for there was no air or wind in the kingdom of the dead. Just as there were good men and bad on earth, so there were good and bad souls in the Underworld, and evil-intentioned and well-intentioned funerary deities. Ra, or rather Auf, had to be defended against the onslaughts of the evil spirits, who often took the form of monstrous serpents, but he always succeeded in emerging into the life of a new day. Osiris, in the early stages, was thought of as one of those spirits of the Underworld who might on one occasion be well-disposed and on another be a threat to the safety of Ra.

As we have seen, the pharaoh was considered in the solar religion to be either the incarnation of Horus the Elder, son of Ra, or the physical son of Ra himself. It was natural therefore to suppose that the pharaoh, like the sun, would be resurrected after death provided the evil spirits of the Underworld were pacified. One of the essential conditions for the continued life of the soul after death was believed, from primitive times, to be the preservation of the body, so from the earliest days when the Osirian legend was incorporated into the solar religion embalmment was practised. It was thought that this, together with the provision of food, servants and a collection of spells (known to us as the *Book of the Dead*) to ward off any ill-intentioned spirits, would assure the dead king's soul of a safe passage through the twelve provinces of the Underworld and into eternal life. Thus the beliefs about the pharaoh exactly mirrored those about the sun who, as we have noted, was also represented as an embalmed body in the night-barque. The gods which formed the crew of the solar boat were enjoined in prayers to defend the soul of the dead pharaoh also.

Osiris as the Symbol of Resurrection

The new pharaoh, being the chief priest as well as the descendant or embodiment of Horus, was naturally prominent in the ritual associated with the death of his father. This, combined with the ever-growing popularity of the Osiris cult, may help to explain how he came to be confused with the other example of filial piety in the Egyptian pantheon, namely Horus, son of Osiris. As a result of this identification, the burial rites of the pharaohs were now associated not only with the daily re-birth of the sun, but also with the resurrection of Osiris – himself once an earthly king – as king in the after-world. Just as the resurrection of Osiris was contingent on the estab-lishment on the throne of his son Ho-rus, so the assumption of power of the new pharaoh was the signal for, and was confirmed by, the passing of the old pharaoh into eternal life. It may be conjectured that this double identification would confer double assurance of life in the afterlife.

At this stage the most stressed aspect of the Osiris myth relating to Horus may have been his concern to reclaim his kingdom from the usurper Set, rather than that of his wish to avenge the murder of his father. It seems that the chief issue in the 'Great Quarrel' was whether Set or Horus should have the throne, i.e. whether the claims of seniority or of descent should have priority in matters of land tenure. At this phase in the de-velopment of Osirian beliefs it would seem that a balance had been struck. Both Osiris and Ra were invoked in the funerary rites of the pharaoh and each was deemed to have power in the land of the dead.

Perhaps the crucial circumstance which assured the further develop-ment of the Osiris cult was the col-lapse of the centralised government at the end of the Sixth Dynasty (2258 B.C.). In the political uncertainty that followed, intellectual activity flour-ished and many old assumptions were questioned. The burial rites accorded to the pharaoh had already been ex-tended to his immediate family and the aristocracy, but from this time on they were increasingly adopted by the common people. The solar ritual was obviously more suited to the king than to any of his subjects. His life

Above. Funerary stela from the tomb of Ramose. Elaborate funeral rites were practised in which the family of the deceased played an important part, each member imitating the role of one of the gods who performed the obsequies of Osiris. Here the brother of the dead man pours a libation. Nineteenth Dynasty, c. 1300 B.C. Ägyptisches Museum, East Berlin.

Opposite. Papyrus showing Osiris as a dark-skinned king swathed in mummy wrappings, enthroned and wearing the *atef* crown and *uraeus*. He gave to those who passed the final ordeal his name and the blessings of eternal felicity. The papyrus is liberally adorned with lotus flowers, symbols of rebirth. Bibliothéque Nationale, Paris.

was open to ritual practices and could be ordered in a semblance of the solar cycle. Besides this, as chief priest of Ra, the pharaoh had obvious connec-tions with him; the common people were unable to approach the inner sanctuary of Ra's temples.

But all men die, leaving behind grieving relatives; it was far easier for the common man to identify himself with Osiris. In addition to all this, we have shown how the cult of the sun-god was bound up with laws about the ownership and inheritance of power or property; it explained the political order of the present world. The Osiris myth, on the other hand, was one which appealed powerfully to the basic human emotions. Its strength was founded in the first in-stance on the pathos of a good man being murdered by his evil brother

but eventually attaining eternal life through the unceasing efforts of his loving wife. Osiris was a man who suffered injustice; his nature was pas-sive. The ordinary man could identify his own destiny with that of Osiris where he was quite unable to identify it with that of the creator god.

At the same time the connection of Osiris with fertility was revived – or perhaps born for the first time. Just as human beings could hope for life after death through Osiris, so through him plant and animal life were con-stantly renewed. It need hardly be stressed that in an agricultural land such as Egypt, where the seasons pre-sent dramatic changes and the whole population is dependent on the nature of these, it was only natural that the chief god should become associated with cosmic forces. Such, no doubt, was originally the concept behind the solar religion, though it later acquired other, political connotations through association with the royal house. As the Osiris cult spread, so it usurped functions of the sun cult.

Equally important in the natural cycle of Egyptian agriculture was the Nile, whose floodwaters dramatically brought life to the parched land. Osiris accordingly became identified with the Nile. Just as Ra had once been considered the supreme self-generative principle, so now Osiris became the tutelary deity of the fertile lands of the Nile valley, the god of floods and vegetation. A common practice became to fill a mummy-shaped linen case with corn seed, to water it and to let the seedlings grow through the linen. The representation was known as the 'Corn Osiris'. In the myth, Osiris's body was enclosed in a tamarisk tree, which grew to an enormous size – a sign of the god's power to bring fertility.

It was perhaps at this stage that Set came to be considered the personifi-cation not simply of contentiousness and low cunning or, in the political interpretation, of Upper Egypt sub-jected to Lower Egypt, but of the de-sert, of storms and of barrenness. For he was now no longer the adversary of Horus, son of Ra; he had assumed the role of adversary of Horus, chief

upholder of the dignity and rights of Osiris, and the murderer of Osiris himself.

It has been remarked that fertility cults are often associated by agricultural peoples with the cult of the dead. Osiris's growth as a fertility-god may therefore have reinforced his claims as funerary divinity. The spread of the burial rites to the whole people seems, however, to have been the decisive factor in determining the further growth of the Osiris cult at the expense of the solar religion. All men, not just the king, now hoped that they would enjoy eternal life, and Osiris was the means by which they hoped to achieve it. Osiris had by now lost his character of frightening spirit of the Underworld: his example represented hope.

True to their traditions, the Egyptians did not entirely discard their former beliefs, and to some extent they still felt it necessary to pacify Osiris – as we shall see, Osiris was also the judge of souls, and had to be satisfied that the dead man was sufficiently virtuous to be admitted. But the chief

hope of survival in the afterlife was to identify completely with the passion of Osiris and to copy the exact forms of his embalmment.

Embalmment and Burial Rites

From the moment of death the deceased's name was prefaced with the name 'Osiris'. The ancient Egyptians would refer to a dead man as 'Osiris X' just as we might say 'the late X'. The ritual embalmment usually took about seventy days and was a very complicated process. Its degrading aspects were certainly considered to be the dead man's way of partaking in the passion of Osiris. The dead man's body was taken away from his home to a special workshop in the form of a tent which was called 'the good house', or 'the place of purification', or 'the house of gold'. First the body was washed with Nile water. Then an incision was made in the left side and the liver, lungs, stomach and intestines were removed.

These organs were placed in four vessels called Canopic jars and their place in the body was taken by spices and resins, though from the Middle Kingdom onwards balls of linen were more commonly used. At this period the brain, too, was removed through the nostrils and the cavity filled with linen or with mud. The purpose of the linen padding was to preserve the features intact; it was believed that if they disintegrated the *ka* or personality would also disintegrate. The heart was left in the body, for it was the seat of the intelligence. The body was preserved in precious oils and resins – though after the religious democratisation this method was practised only for the pharaohs and the very exalted, the cheaper method of soaking in salt (natron) or quicklime being used for others. Amulets were placed on the body, one of the most important being a scarab, placed over the heart; this symbol of renewed life was intended to stimulate the rebirth into eternal life. The body was then wrapped in linen bandages and put in the coffin. All the materials used in embalmment were believed to have grown from the tears shed by the gods at the death of Osiris, and their use in the embalming rites therefore conferred on the dead man the power of these gods.

The processes were simplified over the centuries as a result of the democratisation of the afterlife. Few outside the royal house could afford the elaborate processes of the traditional burials. Thus the viscera were no longer removed in the New Kingdom. The use of Canopic jars became a formality, and eventually not even the jars were placed in the tomb. All that remained of the custom was the placing beside the mummy of figurines of the fours sons of Horus.

The embalmers took the roles of the gods who had helped Isis embalm Osiris. They were led by 'Anubis' and were identified with the sons of Horus and of Khentekhtay. Female mourners, usually the wife of the deceased and a female relative, but on occasion priestesses, impersonated Isis and Nephthys and kept watch over the body until burial. According to the original

Osiris legend, Isis had to guard her husband's body until Horus regained the throne, for until then he would be dead; his resurrection was impossible until Horus had avenged him. The relatives of the dead man therefore had an especial duty to attend in every detail to the prescribed rites — not only for love of the deceased, but because if they neglected their duties he might become an evil demon in the Underworld able to cause harm, especially to their children.

After the prescribed lamentations the mourners set off with the coffin to take it to the tomb. A great procession was formed headed by the coffin lying in a boat and drawn along on a sledge by men and oxen. At either end of the coffin knelt the two chief women mourners, taking the roles of Isis and Nephthys and called 'kites' after the form sometimes assumed by these goddesses. Behind the coffin walked the male mourners. Then came another sledge with the Canopic jars, whose stoppers were plain in the Old Kingdom, had portraits of the deceased in the Middle Kingdom, and

showed the heads of the four sons of Horus thereafter. Finally came the other women, some of them professional mourners, crying out their lamentations. Priests took part in the procession as they did in the actual embalmment. The procession was brought up in the rear by servants bearing the things which the deceased was supposed to need in the next

world. These included food, clothes, furniture and paintings or models of his household servants and other necessities of life. It was thought that the presence of these in the tomb would ensure their provision for the dead man in the next world. For similar reasons the tumulus which surmounted the tomb was shaped rather like a house or, in the case of a king,

like a palace. This practice can be attributed to beliefs in magic powers similar to those of speech and writing, which in the form of papyri or wall-paintings were also provided to ward off evil spirits and to state the dead man's case before his divine judge.

Also carried in the procession were statues of the deceased slightly less than life-size, which represented his *ka* or protective genius. The *ka* was the transcendent part of a man, which rose up from him as he breathed his last and travelled to the West, where he was welcomed by Hathor, given food and drink, and met by his double, or heavenly *ka*. Thereafter the *ka* came to dwell beside the mummy in the tomb, the 'house of the *ka*', and would perish if not provided with nourishment by the family of the deceased. At the same time, however, it dwelt in heaven. The *ka* has to be distinguished from the *ba*, usually translated as the 'soul', which took

the form of a human-headed falcon and was the part of a man that came into existence when he died. The *ba* also occasionally revisited the tomb, especially at night, for the dead body was its rightful dwelling-place.

The *ka* figures were represented as mummies in the Middle Kingdom. In the New Kingdom they were merged with the figures of servants and became the *ushabti* figures, modelled in the likeness of the deceased and inscribed with his name, which were intended to perform in his stead the manual work required of him in the kingdom of Osiris. In later times numerous *ushabtis* as well as protective amulets were enclosed in each tomb, placed alongside the mummy together with the Canopic jars.

The procession made its way towards the burial ground, which was often on the far, western bank of the Nile. They would therefore have to cross the river, where they would ritually re-enact journeys actually taken by the pharaoh's funeral procession to the chief cult centres of Osiris at Busiris and at Abydos. Dancers and musicians joined the procession at the tomb.

Here, the mummy was placed upright and the ceremony of 'Opening of the Mouth' was performed. This corresponded to the occasion of Horus's visit to his father after he had finally been awarded the throne, and by ousting Set had avenged his father's murder. Horus came to perform three tasks: to announce his victory to his father; to present him with the symbol of that victory, which was the

eye that Set snatched out in their battle, and which had been presented to Horus in sign of his victory; and to 'open his mouth'. To do this, Horus touched his father's lips with an adze which represented the Great Bear and with which, in an ancient myth, Set had opened the mouths of the gods, i.e. given them their power of command. When Horus had performed these three tasks his father was woken from his unconsciousness, and the resurrection of his soul was achieved. Similarly, in the burial rites, the ceremony of 'Opening of the Mouth' was performed in order, ritually, to open the way for the rebirth of the deceased's soul.

In the Old Kingdom gilded plaster masks in the likeness of the deceased were placed over the face of the mummy which was then put in a plain wooden coffin, and after the Opening of the Mouth ceremony was laid in the burial vault hollowed out in the rock underneath the sandy desert. Occasionally a stone sarcophagus would be used to give further protection.

When the Middle Kingdom brought simplified embalming techniques, the wooden coffins became more elaborate, the first one being carved in human form and then placed in a second, box-like coffin, on which the spells and incantations earlier carved in stone were now simply painted. In the Twenty-first Dynasty gilded portrait masks gave way to painting of the actual face of the deceased, after it had been padded out as described above. Sometimes

Right. Model of the sacred barge which carried the deceased to the other world, similar to the solar barque and to that which was actually used to take pharaohs across the Nile to the necropolis at Abydos or at Thebes. Prow and stern are fashioned in the form of the head of Hathor, nourisher of the dead, and a solar Eye can be seen on the bow. Twelfth Dynasty.

Below. Mourners at the funeral of Ani. Members of the deceased's family were usually augmented in the vital mourning rituals by professional wailing women. Papyrus of Ani. Nineteenth Dynasty. British Museum, London.

three or more coffins, one inside the other, were used, the better to withstand decay.

In the Late Period, when bitumen was used to preserve the body, it had to be still further covered, for it was black and brittle. The custom was introduced in the Twenty-sixth Dynasty of painting the portrait of the deceased on cartonnage, stiffened canvas placed over the face. In Ptolemaic times these were further elaborated with plaster moulding and the addition of precious stones or glass to represent eyes and jewellery. Finally in Roman times the cartonnage was replaced by a simple wooden panel held in place by the linen bandages and painted with a portrait of the deceased. At this time the bandaging was applied in beautiful patterns, for the mummy was kept on view in the house of the bereaved.

The Judgement of the Dead

Provided that the family meticulously observed the rites of embalmment, the dead man's soul would at least get as far as the hall of judgement in the Underworld. There he would be answerable for himself. Previously, many of the spells employed in funerary papyri were intended to disarm the gods invoked – either, seemingly, by flattery; or by vigorous assertion that the dead man had faithfully worshipped the god concerned; or again by magic spells whereby, like Isis in the legend of the serpent poisoning

Ra, the dead man got the better of the god – rendering him impotent by trickery. Such practices persisted towards the other gods – though to a much lesser degree – but tricks were rarely played on Osiris, who came to be regarded as a just and kindly king, the principle of good who through his son had triumphed over Set, the principle of evil.

Horus, when he came before the tribunal of the gods in the dispute with Set, was eventually given a favourable verdict and awarded the kingdom because he was found to be 'true of voice', that is, honourable or innocent of the charges laid against him by Set. Likewise, according to some versions of the story, the dead Osiris, supported by Isis and Nephthys, was made to come forward for trial at the same hearing, and he too was found to be 'true of voice'. In order that the dead man should be completely identified with every stage of the Osiris myth, it was imagined

that his soul, too, was judged in the Underworld. It was no longer sufficient for the priests to recite magic spells or for the body to be accompanied by a papyrus containing such spells; since the cult had spread to benefit everyone, not just the divine pharaoh, it was thought that eternal life and happiness had to be earned by righteousness.

Judgement of souls may in early times have been thought of as the prerogative of Ra, who later installed Geb and then Thoth as presiding judge; but certainly from the Eighteenth Dynasty onwards the judge of the dead was considered to be Osiris, 'the Good One', redeemer and judge who awaited his 'son who came from earth'. Osiris was pictured as being seated on a throne in a great hall of judgement called the 'Hall of the Two Truths'. The throne stood at the top of a flight of steps which represented the primeval hill on which originally Ra had been born and had begun

creation, but which later came to be associated with the resurrection in the afterlife – one example of how Osiris usurped the attributes of the sun-god. The throne itself was enclosed within a shrine in the form of a wooden coffin decorated like the thrones of the pharaohs with *uraeus* serpents and with the hawk-headed Seker (identified with Osiris) on the top of its lid. Osiris, sitting on the throne, was dressed in a tightly fitting robe of feathers, symbol of righteousness. He had all the insignia of royalty and of divinity: the *atef* crown or white crown and feathers, the royal crooked sceptre and whip, and also the *uas* sceptre, carried only by the gods. His face was coloured green – a reference to his function as god of fertility. Behind him stood Isis and Nephthys and in front of him the fours sons of Horus, Imset, Hapy, Duamutef and Qebhsenuf, the guardians of the Canopic jars. Anubis was also in attendance.

All around the hall were forty-two judges, human-headed mummies each with the feather of Truth on his head and each holding a sharp-edged knife in his hand. These judges represented the forty-two nomes or provinces of Upper and Lower Egypt and each had the task of examining some special aspect of the deceased's conscience. In addition to these representatives of the provinces were the 'Great Ennead' and the 'Little Ennead'. The 'Great Ennead' were all seated on their own thrones and consisted of the sun-god Ra-Harakhte, sitting in his barque with, behind him, his other form, Atum, and the other gods of the Heliopolitan Ennead: Shu, Tefnut, Geb, Nut, Isis, Nephthys and Horus. Osiris did not reappear among these deities; the ninth deity was Hathor. They were attended by Hu ('Authoritative Utterance') and Sia ('Intelligence'), whom we have met before as attendants in the solar barque. The 'Little Ennead' were bearded deities associated with funerary ritual.

When, thanks to the talismans placed on his mummy and especially thanks to the passwords written on the indispensable *Book of the Dead* with which he was furnished, the deceased had safely crossed the terrifying stretch of country between the

Above. Detail from Chapter 146 of the *Book of the Dead*, in which the deceased addresses the seven doors and ten gates of the House of Osiris in the Field of Reeds. Each of the seven doors was guarded by three beings, and no-one could enter without reciting all their names. Each of the ten gates or pylons was in the care of a god and a doorkeeper who also had to be addressed by name and told of all the acts of purification the deceased had performed. Only then could the deceased proceed to the realm of eternal bliss. Papyrus of Ani. Nineteenth Dynasty, 1250 B.C. British Museum, London.

Opposite above. Mummy with the gilded plaster mask used until the Twenty-first Dynasty being placed upright for an offering of water, part of the Opening of the Mouth Ceremony which ritually opened the way for the soul's rebirth. Tomb of Nebamun and Ipuky. Eighteenth Dynasty, 1380 B.C. British Museum, London.

Opposite below. Granite coffin lid of Meri-Mes, Amenhotep III's viceroy in Kush, or Nubia. Kush came under the suzerainty of Egypt in the Eleventh and Twelfth Dynasties. Viceroys supervised the collection of tribute, vital to the Egyptian economy in the Eighteenth Dynasty. The Kushites were culturally absorbed and about 710 B.C. emerged to found the Twenty-fifth Dynasty and 'save' Egyptian civilisation. Eighteenth Dynasty. British Museum, London.

land of the living and the kingdom of the dead, he was immediately ushered into the presence of his sovereign judge by Anubis, or by Horus, or by Mayet. After he had kissed the threshold he entered the 'Hall of the Two Truths', or 'Hall of Double Justice', possibly so-called because a figure of Mayet stood at either end of it. This seat of judgement was situated between the fifth and sixth divisions of the Duat or Underworld.

The trial began with the recitation of the so-called 'negative confession'. The deceased confidently addressed each of his judges in turn, calling him by name to prove that he knew him and had nothing to fear: that he was guilty of no evil actions or qualities in respect of that assessor's special sin. No admission of any sin was made, and the deceased affirmed that he was truly pure. This, the first part of the examination, would seem to be akin to the older practices towards the gods, where it was permissible – and possible – to deceive them. The strong affirmation that the soul of the deceased was without sin seems to have been regarded, like a magic

spell, as sufficient to make it sinless. A spell has been preserved for preventing the heart from betraying the soul in its deceitfulness before the divine judges.

The later beliefs, associated particularly with the Osiris cult, that it was necessary for the soul really to be virtuous, are represented in the second part of the judicial hearing. The existence of these two conceptions of the significance of the judgement may be the reason for the name of the seat of judgement – Hall of the Two Truths.

The second part of the hearing was presided over by Thoth, god of wisdom and reason – who, of course, had been instrumental in persuading the tribunal of the gods of the innocence of Osiris and of Horus. In the centre of the hall was a vast balance surmounted by a baboon, symbol of the god Thoth. Beside the balance stood Mayet, personification of the spirit of justice or of world order, and Anubis, who observed the scales to see if the pans balanced and to make sure that the heart used no trickery. Meanwhile a baboon representing

Thoth made sure that the heart had a fair chance to justify itself. Other figures grouped about the balance were spirits closely connected with the life of the deceased: his soul in the shape of a falcon with a man's head; Meshkent, goddess of birth; Shai, fate, or the individual destiny of the deceased; and the nurse-goddess Renenet. These all testified before the judges as to the character of the deceased. Thoth stood by the balance with his scribe's palette, ready to inscribe the verdict as reported by Anubis. This verdict was arrived at independently of the 'negative confession' and seemed to take no notice at all of the deceased's protestations.

In one of the pans of the balance Anubis or Horus placed the figure of Mayet, or else her hieroglyph, an ostrich feather, symbol of truth. In the other he placed the heart of the deceased, which was considered to be the seat of intelligence and thus the instigator of man's actions and his conscience. We do not know whether a sinful heart was heavier or lighter than Truth; only that if the heart was innocent it was equal in weight to Truth. Thoth verified the weight, then wrote the result on his tablets. If Truth and the heart were of equal weight the 'Great Ennead' ratified the favourable verdict, declaring that the innocence of the deceased was proved and that he should not be thrown to Ammut, 'the Devourer' – a hybrid monster, part lion, part hippopotamus, part crocodile – who crouched

Above left. Painted coffin lid of Ankhesnefer, showing the bull of Ament (a symbol of Osiris) carrying the dead man on his back. Above them hovers the deceased's *ba*, which accompanies them to the underworld (Ament) and the hall of judgement. Twenty-sixth Dynasty. British Museum, London.

Above right. Late Ptolemaic mammisi or chamber in which the goddess gave birth to the king, in the grounds of the principal temple of Hathor, at Dendera, c. first century B.C. By Roman times the mother-goddess Hathor, identified with the wife of the reigning pharaoh, was worshipped in conjunction with Horus. She was assimilated to Isis, whose mysteries were celebrated at Dendera.

nearby, waiting to devour the hearts of the guilty.

The goddess Mayet now dressed the deceased in feathers, like Osiris, as a symbol of his righteousness, and he was brought before Osiris by Horus, who announced the verdict to him, pleading that he should be offered bread and beer in the presence of Osiris himself and that he should live like the followers of Horus forever. The deceased himself repeated that he had told no lies and that there was no sin in him, and Osiris declared that he might depart victorious and mingle freely with the gods and the spirits of the dead, assigning to him a holding or homestead in his kingdom.

The deceased, thus justified, would prepare to lead a life of eternal bliss, in the company of an ideal wife who would minister to all his needs. It is true that it would be considered his duty to cultivate the domains of Osiris and keep dykes and irrigation canals in good repair, for the kingdom of the dead was a replica of the Egyptian state in its most favourable aspects. The fields of the blessed were like those of the Delta Region near Sebennytos, fertile and well-watered, and the *Book of the Dead* described the deceased ploughing in a field by the side of a long wide stream in which there were neither fish nor worms. Magic, however, permitted him to avoid physical labour; at burial he would have been provided with *ushabti* or *shawabti* figures ('Answerers') – those little statuettes in stone or glazed composition which have been found in tombs by the hundreds and which, when the dead man was called upon to perform some task, would hasten to take his place and do the job for him. Meanwhile he would be free to sail along the heavenly Nile, play draughts, talk and sing with friends and enjoy the meals provided by his survivors at his tomb.

Later Developments in the Osiris Cult

Osiris must have seemed to the ancient Egyptians a much more accessible god than the solar divinities. No one but the pharaoh could claim to identify with the splendour of the cycle of the sun's death and rebirth. But Osiris was a man who, though just, suffered on earth at the hands of others. He was able to overcome the seeming dissolution of death through his own virtue (he was 'true of voice') and through the loving ministrations of his wife and son. He represented the possibility of rebirth and the power of revival, not only for human beings, but also for plant life. Though dead, he was the source of life.

It is clear that the pharaohs would have no difficulty in identifying the cyclic patterns of their own reigns with the annual death and renewal of the natural world, for it was long believed that if the royal house prospered so would the land and its agriculture. Thus the pharaohs could perhaps claim identity with the personal death and rebirth of Osiris as of right. For the ordinary man, identification with Osiris was more a matter of hope and eventually of deserts: under the spread of the Osirian beliefs to the mass of the people, the Egyptian religion became less a collection of magic spells against the evil

intentions of various deities and propitiation of the good deities, than an ethical system which laid down a code of conduct in this life on which would depend eternal salvation in the next.

Under Osirian influence the Egyptian religion became an optimistic one, which held out hope for every man. This in itself may account for the rapid growth in the importance of Osiris at the expense of Ra. Not all the solar beliefs were abandoned, but they were incorporated into the Osiris cult, just as once Osiris had been incorporated into the Heliopolitan system. The sun-god retained his cult, as Amon-Ra, until the early fourth century B.C., but by Ptolemaic times he was neglected.

In the process of acquiring these extra functions, however, the character of Osiris himself changed. This change was partly due to absorption of features which properly belonged to the sun-god; but it was also due from Ptolemaic times onwards to confusion or coalescence with foreign gods.

The association of both Osiris and Isis with fertility cults was increasingly stressed from the New Kingdom onwards, and this encouraged their gradual penetration into the world of the living. Osiris now tended to become ruler of this world as well as of the Underworld and the hieroglyph for his name from the Twentieth Dynasty onwards was the solar disk rather than the eye.

The sacred bull Apis, a fertility-god recognised by peculiar markings, had become widely venerated in the New Kingdom period, when he was considered to be a manifestation of Ptah, the creator god. As each bull died, another was found to take his place, and the funeral rites were not unlike those of a king, who in the same way always has a natural successor who was accorded the same veneration as his predecessor. Like a king, or any other man who received the burial rites, Apis was identified with Osiris. He soon became so closely associated with him that a new hybrid god came into being, called Usar-Hape, the Egyptian form of the two names. The

Above. A statue of the Roman period of Isis, mother of all things. Among the most ancient of the Egyptian deities, Isis also survived the longest, and was popular in Rome. Here she bears a Roman cornucopia. In Egypt, her mysteries were celebrated especially at Dendera, Esna, Edfu and Philae. Musei Vaticani.

Opposite. Sennofer and his sister Merit. From the tomb of Sennofer at Thebes. Sennofer holds to his nostrils the lotus, symbol of rebirth from which sprang Ra and Nefertum. His seat rises from the midst of the Tree of Heaven, whose fruits are the food of the great gods and give them immortality. The tombs of the royal servants, while not as magnificent as those of their masters, often yield artistic treasures. Sennofer cared for the royal gardens and parks during the reign of Thuthmosis III. Eighteenth Dynasty.

———————————

Greeks living at Memphis in the Late Period adopted this deity as Osorapis, and also worshipped Isis and Anubis. It was Osorapis whom Ptolemy I chose to be the official god of Egypt and Greece, which he hoped to unify. The name of the new god was Serapis or Sarapis and he was represented in statues looking rather like Pluto with long hair and beard, seated on a throne with the triple-headed dog Cerberus at his feet. He was a very popular god and, though an artificial

creation, his cult rapidly spread. The full circle of his development was complete when, in the third century A.D., Serapis once more became a sort of solar deity. His importance as state god introduced him into the sun cult associated since the beginning of Egyptian history with the pharaonic power.

This may be said to mark the end of the Egyptian religion in its native form. Though the priests tried to encourage animal-worship as being the most essentially Egyptian element in the religion, foreign influence could not be eradicated. As the cult of Osiris or Serapis spread throughout the Greek world, so did that of Isis and of Horus the Child, or Harpokrates, as he was called in Greek. Isis became the chief female deity, but in the character of a mother-goddess, and she was generally depicted suckling the child Harpokrates. It is thought by some that excessive veneration of the Virgin and Child by early Christians may owe something to the influence of this widespread cult in the Roman Empire. It was resisted by the early Roman emperors, for she had been the goddess of Cleopatra, but in the reign of Caligula a temple dedicated to Isis was built near Rome and under Vespasian she and Serapis appeared on imperial coins. Caracalla had a temple of Isis built in Rome itself. Hathor, Sebek and Imhotep were also worshipped in the Empire and the Egyptian deities spread to every part of it.

The Egyptian gods may have owed much of their popularity outside Egypt and their strength in the face of other deities within Egypt to the sure faith they offered of life after death. The Greek and Roman deities had become figures in stylised myths which bore comparatively little relation to the everyday concerns of their worshippers. The myths were stories told largely for entertainment and the gods depicted in them lacked mystery. The Egyptian deities, on the other hand, even during the Graeco-Roman period, never lost their symbolic associations with the all-important cycles of birth and death, agelessly significant.

Chronology of Ancient Egypt

Date B.C.*	Dynasty	Important Pharaohs	Political and Social Developments	Religious and Mythological Developments. Texts	Monuments (extant)
Dates unknown	Predynastic Period		Probable first unification of Egypt by followers of Ra: capital at Heliopolis	Sun-cult associated henceforth with royal power. Tribal hunting or warrior gods acquired characteristics suited to agricultural people: deities of earth, water, rain, sky. Cults of Min, Osirian sed-festivals, Horus as warrior falcon-god, probably of Libyan origin.	
ARCHAIC PERIOD					
3100 - 2884	1	Menes (Narmer) Djer		Proximity of Abydos to Thinis promotes interplay of Osirian and Horus myths. Capital at Memphis promotes Ptah as supreme creator god; Ra, Horus, Hathor, especially in royal sun cult. Pharaoh identified with Horus; dead pharaoh with Osiris.	Narmer Palette from Hierakonpolis. Mastabas (mud-brick flat tombs) of early pharaohs at Saqqara, near Memphis.
2884 - 2780	2			Style of representing deities largely fixed.	
2780 - 2680	3	Djoser Huny Sneferu	Advanced shipbuilding; trade with Phoenicia (see Osiris/Isis myth). Victories against Nubia. Copper-mining in Sinai.	Mortuary ritual established, including mummification. Solar cults largely exclusive to ruling dynasty.	First stone monuments: Step Pyramid of Djoser at Saqqara. Pyramid of Sneferu at Maidum.
OLD KINGDOM OR PYRAMID AGE					
2680 - 2565	4	Cheops (Khufu) Khephren (Khafre) Mykerinus (Menkaure)	Unified organisation of society – developed agricultural techniques permit large-scale enterprises such as pyramid-building.	Royal pyramid tombs symbolic of primeval hill.	'Great Pyramids' of Cheops, Khephren and Mykerinus at Giza. Great Sphinx at Giza, probably built by Khephren.
2565 - 2420	5	Userkaf Sahure Niussere Unis	Stable government and prosperity. Tools and weapons of copper. Use of gold, silver, lapis lazuli, turquoise. Barter system: no money. Development of astronomy, engineering (for building and irrigation).	Strengthening of royal solar cult. Pharaoh identified with composite god Ra-Harakhte. Wife of Heliopolitan High Priest identified with Hathor; temple musicians 'the god's concubines'. Heliopolitan cosmogony. Pyramid Texts first appear during reign of Unis (Heliopolitan recension).	Obelisk temples to the sun ('Benben stone'). Mastaba of Tiy at Saqqara: paintings and reliefs with scenes of daily life. Pyramid of Unis at Saqqara.
2420 - 2258	6	Pepi I Pepi II (last of dynasty)	Power of pharaohs gradually weakens (from late Fifth Dynasty): they become feudal lords; provincial governors gain strength, their office becomes hereditary.	Pyramid Texts elaborated. Cult of pharaoh as god. Cults of cyclic change and seasonal fertility; Apep serpent daily reconquered. Tipping balance against evil a communal effort under pharaoh.	
FIRST INTERMEDIATE PERIOD					
2258 - 2225	7 8		Foreign invasions. Civil disorder and fragmentation. Provincial governors exploit local cult allegiances to seize power locally. Wealth and artistic expertise attenuated but old traditions partially maintained.	Cult of ram-headed Harsaphes as state deity and god of fertility.	
2225 - 2134	9 10		Capital at Heracleopolis in Middle Egypt. Rivalry leading to fighting between nobles, esp. those of Heracleopolis and Thebes.	Intellectual/theological ferment. Hopes for life after death extended to non-royal individuals. Literature flourished despite political troubles: Instruction for King Merykare, Admonitions of Ipuwer.	
2134 - 2000	11		Princes of Thebes conquered and reunited whole country. Capital at Thebes in Upper Egypt. Establishment of 'Middle Kingdom'.	Mont as protective deity of kingdom.	Tombs of Princes of Beni Hassan in Middle Egypt (20 km south of Minya): murals of daily life – 11th and 12th Dynasties.
MIDDLE KINGDOM					
2000 - 1786	12	Amenemhet I Sesostris I Amenemhet II Sesostris II Sesostris III Amenemhet III Amenemhet IV	Capital at Lisht near Memphis. Continued importance of local governors, aristocracy, priesthoods. Decentralisation enabled Egypt to survive outside attack, esp. by Nubians and Asiatic nomads. System of co-regency from Amenemhet II onwards. International trade important. Nubia (Kush) under Egyptian rule. Turquoise mining expanded in Sinai. Irrigation and land drainage developed (Faiyum) by Amenemhet III. General prosperity. Temple architecture more elaborate, showy, less refined than in Old Kingdom.	Book of the Dead, enshrining already archaic beliefs. Development of beliefs on Judgement of the Dead. Amon emerged as major Theban god: cult of composite deity, Amon-Ra. Sebek god of the pharaohs. The Story of Sinuhe composed.	Pyramid of Sesostris II, south of Faiyum. Pyramid and Labyrinth (funerary temple) of Amenemhet III at Hawara (Faiyum oasis). Thebes: Great Temple of Karnak begun (took more than 1,000 years to complete). Complex of temples dedicated to Amon, Mut and Khons a stronghold of Amon-Ra priesthood.
SECOND INTERMEDIATE PERIOD (Dynasties 13 and 14 sometimes included in Middle Kingdom)					
1786 - 1650	13 14	Theban rulers Lords of Xoic, in Delta.	Upper and Lower Egypt separate. Foreign invaders successful against Egypt because their power was based on Bronze Age chariot warfare.	Coffin Texts, based on Book of the Dead and Pyramid Texts.	
1650 - 1570	15	Hyksos ('Shepherd Kings')	Hyksos, probably from Syria, overran all parts of Egypt. Capital at Avaris, in Delta.	Hyksos hated as foreign kings but they adopted Egyptian ways and cults. The warlike Set their favoured god.	Hyksos Sphinx at Tanis, in Delta.
?	16	Hyksos	Uncertain: may have been continuous with 15th Dynasty; or contemporary with 13th Dynasty.		
c. 1600 - 1570	17	Theban rulers Kemose (last of dynasty)	Thebes regained power locally (note overlapping dates). 1570: Theban revolt expelled Hyksos.		

Date B.C.*	Dynasty	Important Pharaohs	Political and Social Developments	Religious and Mythological Developments. Texts	Monuments (extant)
NEW KINGDOM					
1570 - c. 1305	18 First Empire	Ahmose I (Amasis I) Thuthmosis I Thuthmosis II *with* Q. Hatshepsut Thuthmosis III Amenhotep (Amenophis) II Thuthmosis IV Amenhotep III Amenhotep IV (Akhenaten: *wife* Nefertiti) Smenkare Tutankhamon Ai Horemheb	Resistance of local governors to Thebans quelled; they became mere administrators. Egypt re-established as a military, expansionist state. Thuthmosis I made imperial conquests in Asia; also in Kush (Nubia). Thuthmosis III established empire in Asia stretching beyond Euphrates. Amenhotep II also warrior-king and sportsman. Amenhotep III: reign peaceful and magnificent. Increased wealth used in monuments; influx of gold from Nubia, silver, ivory, etc. Imperial conquests lost under Akhenaten.	Mother of Ahmose I claimed as wife of Amon-Ra, now principal royal god. New religious influences following Asian excursions; interest in Asiatic gods and in monotheism, leading eventually to experiment with Atenism (solar monotheism) under Amenhotep IV (renamed Akhenaten). *Tell el Amarna Tablets*, account of reigns of Amenhotep III and Akhenaten. Violent reaction and repression of Atenism. Conservatism further entrenched, in belief and art. Supremacy of Amon-Ra priesthood of Thebes secured by Horemheb.	Theban necropolis developed: Valley of the Kings – tombs tunnelled in high rock face above west bank of Nile. Tombs of Amenhotep II, Thuthmosis III, Tutankhamon and Horemheb. Valley of the Nobles (incl. tomb of Sennofer), and Valley of the Queens – smaller tombs cut in rock face. Temple of Hatshepsut at Deir el-Bahri. Temple of Thuthmosis III at Medinet Habu. Colossi of Memnon (two 70-foot statues of Amenhotep III). Temple of Amon at Luxor, built by Amenhotep III, linked to larger Great Temple of Karnak by 2 km avenue of sphinxes Serapeum begun for burial of Apis bulls at Saqqara. Akhenaten's Palace and rock-cut tombs at Tell el Amarna.
c. 1320 - 1200	19 Second Empire	Rameses I Seti I Rameses II (wife Nefertari) Merenptah Seti II	Military dynasty. Seti I reconquers lost lands in Syria. Debilitating conflicts with Hittites under Rameses II. Each claimed victory at Kadesh. Rameses II built extensively, using forced labour, incl. Israelites (time of the Flight from Egypt). He moved capital from Memphis to Tanis, city of god Set. 1220–1165: Three waves of would-be invaders ('Peoples of the Sea'), armed with Iron Age weaponry, barely repelled.	Strengthening of native cultural tradition. Beneficent role of Set as warlike defender of the ruling house stressed. Weakness of pharaohs of 19th-21st Dynasties allowed establishment of theocracy by Amon-Ra priesthood at Thebes.	Thebes: Valley of Kings – tomb of Seti I. Abydos: Osireion – temple of Seti I, containing Gallery of Kings (king-list from Menes) – temple of Rameses II. Rock Temples at Abu Simbel, begun by Seti I, completed by Rameses II (four colossi). Now moved to west of Lake Nasser, formed by Aswan High Dam above First Cataract: Great Temple dedicated to Amon-Ra, smaller temple dedicated to Hathor, in honour of Nefertari. Thebes: Valley of Queens – tomb of Nefertari. Necropolis – Rameseum (funerary temple of Rameses II). Memphis: Colossal statue of Rameses II; alabaster sphinx of Rameses II
1190 - 1085	20	Rameses III *with* Tiy Rameses IV – XI	Rameses III united factions in Egypt to repel confederation of Sea Peoples, probably Philistines, Greeks, Sardinians and Sicilians. Relative decline of Egypt as a world power thereafter. Turned inward politically to maintain status quo. Capital at Tanis.	Adherence to archaic beliefs and copying of Old Kingdom styles, e.g. in sculpture. Under Rameses XI High Priest of Amon-Ra, Herihor, virtually independent ruler of south. *Tale of Wenamun*.	Temple of Rameses III at Medinet Habu, near Thebes: scenes of Rameses's victories against Sea Peoples. Thebes: Valley of the Kings – tombs of Rameses III, Rameses VI, Rameses IX.
LATE DYNASTIC PERIOD	*(Dynasties 21 and 22 sometimes included in New Kingdom)*				
1085-945	21	*Tanite Dynasty* Smendes (at Tanis) Herihor (at Thebes)	Upper and Lower Egypt effectively divided: Priest-kings' capital at Thebes in opposition to pharaohs at Tanis.		
945 - c. 750	22	*Libyan Dynasty* Sheshonq I	Growing strength of Delta region: Libyans seized throne. Capital at Bubastis.	Libyan pharaohs adopted Delta goddess Bast as their state deity and tried to fuse her with Sekhmet. Sheshonq I had his son appointed High Priest of Amon-Ra, thus re-uniting the country.	Shrine of Bast at Thebes. Additions to Bast temples at Bubastis.
c. 750 - c. 720 c. 720 - c. 710	23 24	(Little known about these dynasties.)			
c. 710 - 663	25	*Nubian (or Ethiopian) Dynasty* Piankhi Shabaka (Shebteko) Taharko	Egypt conquered by Negroes from Sudan under Piankhi, prince from Napata. Shabaka established capital at Thebes. 675–71: Assyrians under Esarhaddon invade, took Memphis from Taharko. 663: Thebes conquered by Assurbanipal of Assyria. End of Nubian rule.		
663 - 525	26	*Saite Period ('Renaissance')* Necho Psamtik (Psammetichus) I Necho II Psamtik II Apries Ahmose (Amasis) II Psamtik III	Necho, governor of Sais, appointed king by Assyrians. Capital at Sais. c. 650: Iron came into general use in Egypt: associated with Set. Egyptians under Psamtik I expel Assyrians. 612: Overthrow of Assyrian Empire; Egypt shares in partition with Medes and Babylonians. 605: Egypt turned back from Asia by Nebuchadnezzar of Babylon. 586: Judah crushed by Nebuchadnezzar.	Pharaohs supported their rule by Osirian doctrine rather than solar cults. Set becomes personification of evil. Saite revival: recreations of Old Kingdom religion, literature, art and architecture under Psamtik I.	Granite Temple (sarcophagus) for Apis bull at Saqqara.
525 - 404	28	*Achaemenid Rulers*	525: Egypt defeated by Cambyses II of Persia. Achaemenid rule Cambyses II – Darius II. 405: Egypt rebels against Persians.		
404 - 399	27	Amyrtaeus	Dynasty of one pharaoh: capital Sais. N.B. chronology: 27th *after* 28th Dynasty.		
399 - 380	29	Achoris	29th and 30th Dynasties: last native dynasties. Resistance to Persian attacks, with Greek help. Capital Mendes.		
380 - 343	30	Nectanebo (Nekhtnebf) I Takhos Nectanebo II	Capital at Sebennytos. Both Nectanebos resisted Persians and built widely. 341: Persians again win power in Egypt. 332: Alexander the Great conquers Persians, takes Egypt, founds Alexandria. 323: Alexander dies; his general Ptolemy governs Egypt.	Final eclipse of Amon-Ra and all old solar cults.	
305 - 30 B.C.	*Ptolemaic Dynasty*	Ptolemies I – XIV Cleopatra VII	305: Ptolemy named Pharaoh: new dynasty. Egypt's navy dominates E. Mediterranean. 58: Ptolemy XI calls on Rome (Pompey) for support in regaining throne: beginning of Roman power in Egypt. 31: Cleopatra, Ptolemy XI's daughter, tried to exploit love of Caesar and then Marc Antony to regain power for Egypt. Her navy defeated by Rome at Actium. 30: Suicide of Cleopatra and death of her son Caesarion (Ptolemy XIV). Egypt a Roman province.	Osarapis (Serapis) chief state god. After Ptolemy II, pharaohs worshipped as living gods. Cults of afterlife (Isis and Osiris) strengthened by burden on natives of taxation and forced labour to support splendour of Ptolemaic court. Large Jewish population (c. 15%).	Tuna el-Gebel (Hermopolis): tomb of High Priest Petosiris; also necropolis of mummified ibis and baboons (sacred to Thoth). Edfu: Temple of Horus, built 257-237 by Ptolemy III, most complete surviving temple. Esna: Temple of Khnum. Kom Ombo, Upper Egypt: temple dedicated to Sebek and Haroeris by Ptolemy VIII. Dendera: Temple of Hathor (built 116 B.C.-A.D. 34). Contains Chapel of Nut (ceiling); reliefs of Cleopatra and Caesarion.

*using 'Middle Chronology'. N.B. Old Kingdom dates uncertain – allow ± 100 years; from New Kingdom allow ± 10 years.

Further Reading List

Alfred, C. *The Egyptians*. Thames & Hudson, London, 1961.

Brandon, S. G. F. *Creation Legends of the Ancient Near East*. Hodder & Stoughton, London, 1963.

Bonnet, H. *Reallexikon der ägyptischen Religionsgeschichte*. Berlin, 1952.

Budge, E. A. W. *From Fetish to God in Ancient Egypt*. Oxford Univ. Press, 1934.

Budge, E. A. W. *Egyptian Religion*, 1899; pb Routledge & Kegan Paul, 1979.

Cerny, J. *Ancient Egyptian Religion*. Hutchinson, London 1952.

Cooke, H. P. *Osiris. A Study in Myths, Mysteries and Religion*. C. W. Daniel Co., London, 1931.

Desroches-Noblecourt, C. *Tutankhamen*. The Connoisseur & Michael Joseph, London, 1963.

Emery, W. B. *Archaic Egypt*. Penguin Books, Harmondsworth, 1961.

Erman, A. *A Handbook of Egyptian Religion*, 1934.

Frankfort, H. *Ancient Egyptian Religion*. Harper & Bros., New York, 1948.

Frankfort, H. *Kingship and the Gods*. Chicago, 1948.

Frankfort, H. and H. A. (eds.) *The Intellectual Adventure of Ancient Man*.

Chicago, 1946; and as *Before Philosophy*. Penguin Books, Harmondsworth, 1949.

Gardiner, Sir Alan H. *Egypt of the Pharaohs*, Oxford Univ. Press, 1961.

Glanville, S. R. K. *The Legacy of Egypt*. Oxford Univ. Press, 1942.

Griffiths, John Gwyn. *The Conflict of Horus and Seth*. Liverpool Univ. Press, 1960.

Hawkes, Jacquetta. *The First Great Civilisations*. Hutchinson, 1973.

Hawkes, Jacquetta. *Man and the Sun*. Cresset Press, London, 1962.

Herodotus. *The Histories*, trans. by Aubrey de Selincourt. Penguin Classics, Harmondsworth, 1954.

Introductory Guide to the Egyptian Collections. British Museum, London, 1964.

James, E. O. *The Ancient Gods*. Weidenfeld & Nicolson, London, 1960.

James, E. O. *Myth and Ritual in the Ancient Near East*. Thames & Hudson, London, 1958.

James, T. H. *An Introduction to Ancient Egypt*. British Museum Publications, 1979.

McCulloch, J. A. & Gray, Louis H. *Egyptian Mythology* in *The Mythology of All Races*. Cooper Square Pubs. Inc., New York, 1922.

Manchip White, J. E. *Ancient Egypt*. Allen & Unwin.

Mercer, S. A. B. *The Religion of Ancient Egypt*. Luzac & Co., London, 1949.

Murray, M. A. *Ancient Egyptian Legends*. John Murray, London, 1913.

Murray, M. A. *The Splendour that was Egypt*. Sidgwick & Jackson, London, 1949.

Newby, P. H. *The Egypt Story*. Deutsch, 1979.

Plutarch. *Isis and Osiris*. Vol. V in Plutarch's *Moralia* (14 Vols.) Ed & trans. by F. C. Babbitt. Loeb Classical Library, London, 1936.

Rundle Clark, R. T. *Myth and Symbol in Ancient Egypt*. Thames & Hudson, London, 1959; pb 1978.

Sauneron, S. *Quatre Campagnes à Esna*. Publications de l'Institut français d'Archéologie orientale, Cairo, 1959.

Shorter, A. W. *The Egyptian Gods*. Routledge & Kegan Paul, London, 1937.

Shorter, A. W. *An Introduction to Egyptian Religion*. Routledge & Kegan Paul, London, 1931.

Spence, Lewis. *The Myths and Legends of Ancient Egypt*. Harrap, London, 1915.

Wainwright, G. A. *The Sky Religion in Egypt*. Cambridge Univ. Press, 1938.

Acknowledgments

Photographs. Alinari, Florence half-title page, 9 top, 19 right, 29, 52, 53 bottom, 57, 61, 82, 85 top, 93, 108, 109, 133 top, 139; P Almasy, Neuilly-sur-Seine 92; Archives Photographiques, Paris 9 bottom right, 17 top, 25; Archiv für Kunst und Geschichte Berlin 12 left, 69, 91 right, 121; Audrain – Samivel 6; BBC Hulton Picture Library, London 56; Bavaria Verlag, Gauting 96; British Museum, London 20, 40, 41 bottom, 49, 60, 64 right, 75 left, 117 bottom, 120 top, 132 bottom, 133 bottom, 134 bottom, 136 bottom, 137 left; J E Bulloz, Paris 13, 19 left, 128, 132 top; Egyptian Museum, Cairo 12 right; Fitzwilliam Museum, Cambridge 125; Forman Brothers 10, 24, 33, 68, 81, 90, 99 top, 116; Photographic Giraudon, Paris 17 bottom right, 71, 78, 100, 124; Hamlyn Group Picture Library 14 top, 30, 36 right, 41 top, 42, 44 bottom, 48 bottom, 62, 65, 84, 89, 98, 111; Hirmer Fotoarchiv, Munich 26, 35, 46, 50, 51, 58, 70, 87, 102, 123; Michael Holford, Loughton 11, 18, 23 top, 38, 39, 43, 47, 59, 74, 83, 86, 94, 95, 106, 130, 131 top, 134 top, 135; A F Kersting, London 23 bottom; Larousse, Paris 22; Mansell Collection, London 36 left, 53 top, 73, 91 left, 99 bottom, 101, 103, 105, 113, 117 top, 132 bottom, 136 top; Bildarchiv Foto Marburg 14, 17 bottom left, 37, 44 top, 75 right, 76, 80, 85 bottom, 87 bottom, 110, 120 bottom, 129, 137 right; Oropeza 64 left; Paul Popper, London 48 top; Scala, Antella 115; Shell, London 15, 72, 127; Roger-Viollet, Paris 9 bottom left, 32, 66, 77, 97; Roger Wood, London, 2, 27, 31, 54, 55, 67, 79, 107, 118, 119, 138.

Index